Michael Miller

D0878122

Sams **Teach Yourself**

Vine™

in **10 Minutes**

SAMS | 800 East 96th Street, Indianapolis, Indiana 46240

Sams Teach Yourself Vine in 10 Minutes

Copyright © 2014 by Pearson Education, Inc.

All rights reserved. No part of this book shall be reproduced, stored in a retrieval system, or transmitted by any means, electronic, mechanical, photocopying, recording, or otherwise, without written permission from the publisher. No patent liability is assumed with respect to the use of the information contained herein. Although every precaution has been taken in the preparation of this book, the publisher and author assume no responsibility for errors or omissions. Nor is any liability assumed for damages resulting from the use of the information contained herein.

ISBN-13: 978-0-7897-5236-9
ISBN-10: 0-7897-5236-0

Library of Congress Control Number: 2013944070

Printed in the United States of America

First Printing September 2013

Trademarks

All terms mentioned in this book that are known to be trademarks or service marks have been appropriately capitalized. Pearson Education, Inc. cannot attest to the accuracy of this information. Use of a term in this book should not be regarded as affecting the validity of any trademark or service mark.

Warning and Disclaimer

Every effort has been made to make this book as complete and as accurate as possible, but no warranty or fitness is implied. The information provided is on an "as is" basis. The author and the publisher shall have neither liability nor responsibility to any person or entity with respect to any loss or damages arising from the information contained in this book.

Bulk Sales

Pearson Education, Inc. offers excellent discounts on this book when ordered in quantity for bulk purchases or special sales. For more information, please contact

U.S. Corporate and Government Sales
1-800-382-3419
corpsales@pearsontechgroup.com

For sales outside of the U.S., please contact

International Sales
international@pearson.com

Editor-in-Chief
Greg Wiegand

Executive Editor
Rick Kughen

Managing Editor
Kristy Hart

Project Editor
Katie Matejka

Senior Indexer
Cheryl Lenser

Proofreader
Seth Kerney

Technical Editor
Karen Weinstein

Publishing Coordinator
Kristen Watterson

Cover Designer
Mark Shirar

Compositor
Nonie Ratcliff

Table of Contents

About the Author

Michael Miller has written more than 100 non-fiction how-to books over the past two decades, as well as a variety of web articles. His best-selling books include *Que's Absolute Beginner's Guide to Computer Basics*, *Facebook for Grown-Ups*, *My Pinterest*, and *Sams Teach Yourself YouTube in 10 Minutes*. Collectively, his books have sold more than one million copies worldwide.

Miller has established a reputation for clearly explaining technical topics to non-technical readers, and for offering useful real-world advice about complicated topics. More information can be found at the author's website, located at www.molehillgroup.com. He can be contacted via email at vine@molehillgroup.com. His Twitter handle is @molehillgroup.

Dedication

To Sherry, as usual.

Acknowledgments

Thanks to the usual suspects for turning my manuscript into a book, including but not limited to Rick Kughen, Greg Wiegand, Katie Matejka, Seth Kerney, and technical editor Karen Weinstein.

We Want to Hear from You!

As the reader of this book, *you* are our most important critic and commentator. We value your opinion and want to know what we're doing right, what we could do better, what areas you'd like to see us publish in, and any other words of wisdom you're willing to pass our way.

You can email or write us directly to let us know what you did or didn't like about this book—as well as what we can do to make our books stronger.

Please note that we cannot help you with technical problems related to the topic of this book.

When you write, please be sure to include this book's title and author as well as your name and phone or email address. We will carefully review your comments and share them with the author and editors who worked on the book.

Email: consumer@samspublishing.com

Mail: Sams Publishing
         ATTN: Reader Feedback
         800 East 96th Street
         Indianapolis, IN 46240 USA

Reader Services

Visit our website and register this book at informit.com/register for convenient access to any updates, downloads, or errata that might be available for this book.

LESSON 1

What Is Vine—and What Can You Do With It?

In this lesson, you learn all about Vine—the company, the app, and the social network.

Introducing Vine

If you haven't yet heard about Vine, chances are, you will. Vine is a new mobile app and video-sharing service that lets you record short (six-second maximum) looping videos on your mobile home, and then share those videos with online friends.

Vine lets you easily share your videos with friends—or, as the company likes to say, "share life in motion." In a way, Vine is like a video version of Instagram, only instead of sharing still photos, you share Vine's short looping videos. Vine videos (called *vines*) can be viewed from the Vine mobile app, linked to from a person's Twitter feed, shared via Facebook, or embedded in web pages and blogs.

Vine, the company, was founded in June 2012. The company was acquired by Twitter in October 2012 for approximately $30 million. The Vine service (and initial iOS device app) launched publicly on January 24, 2013.

During its short life, Vine has become enormously popular, especially among younger users. Just three months after its release, the Vine app became the number-one free app in Apple's United States App Store, and is used on eight percent of all iOS devices—more than double any other video app. In its first 6 months on the market, Vine's user base grew to more than 13 million users. These users upload more than 2,000 new videos every hour.

What Vine Does

To use Vine, you must download and install the Vine app on your smartphone or tablet. The Vine app is currently available for both Android and iOS devices, including the iPhone, iPad, and iPod touch. You must use your phone or tablet to shoot Vine videos; you can't create Vine videos from your computer.

The Vine app is completely free, as is Vine's accompanying social network. More information is available at the www.vine.co website.

Recording (Short) Videos

The Vine app lets you record short videos using your tablet or smartphone's built-in video camera, as shown in Figure 1.1. Vine videos can be up to six seconds in length, just long enough to make a point or record the moment, but definitely not long enough to count as a full-length home movie.

NOTE: **Six and a Half**

Although Vine makes a big deal of its six-second maximum videos, technically Vine videos are just a tad longer—six and a half seconds, to be exact. That extra half second gives you a little breathing room at the end of the official six-second length.

Why six seconds? Prior to its launch, Vine did a lot of testing on various video lengths, from four seconds to ten seconds. The company determined that four seconds was too short and ten seconds too long for the kind of immediate video sharing it had in mind. Six seconds, on the other hand, was just right in terms of both creation and viewing. By limiting videos to just six seconds, Vine lets you capture the "now" of a moment. In addition, Vine's six-second videos are both easily transmitted (no long uploads or downloads) and quickly grasped by viewers.

FIGURE 1.1 Recording a video with the Vine app.

Note that a Vine video doesn't have to contain a single six-second shot. Recording can be stopped and restarted multiple times within that six-second limit to create a video with multiple shots or scenes.

> **NOTE: Shorter Videos**
> Your videos don't have to last the full six seconds that Vine allows. It's okay to record and share even shorter videos, if you want.

Vine videos are looping videos, which means that you don't have to start or stop them. When you access a video on Vine, the video starts automatically and then repeats endlessly.

Sharing Videos

The Vine videos you shoot with your smartphone or tablet camera are posted to Vine's social network, where they can be searched for (via hashtags in the descriptions) and viewed by other users of the Vine app, as shown in Figure 1.2. You can also share your Vine videos via Twitter and Facebook, as shown in Figure 1.3; when someone clicks the link to a video, that video opens in that person's web browser. This way, you can share your Vine videos with computer users who don't have the Vine app on their phones.

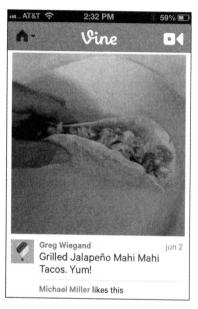

FIGURE 1.2   Viewing a video from the Vine app.

In addition to linking to your Vine videos, you can also embed them in your own website or blog. When someone opens your page or blog post, the Vine video begins to play—and then plays continuously, always looping back to the beginning.

FIGURE 1.3   A link to a Vine video in a Twitter tweet.

What Vine Doesn't Do

Vine isn't a full-featured video-sharing application. It's not like YouTube, which lets you upload long, fully edited videos. There's a lot you *can't* do with Vine.

No Editing

One important thing you can't do with a Vine video is edit it. After you shoot the video, your only options are to post it or delete it. So, if you record something you don't like, delete it and start over. There's no way to edit out mistakes.

Nor is there any way to edit in voiceovers, background music, or special effects. What you shoot is what you get. It's all about recording the moment, not about creating artificial moments.

No Uploading

Vine lets you shoot and share videos directly from your mobile device. You cannot upload pre-existing videos. So, if you have a video stored on your computer or mobile device, you can't upload it to Vine, nor share it with Vine users. Vine is only for newly created Vine videos, period.

How You Can Use Vine

Different people use Vine in different ways. Some people like to shoot and share videos that document their activities, such as attending concerts or birthday parties. Other people use Vine to report newsworthy events and then share those events in near real time. Still others use Vine more creatively, to shoot entertaining or thought-provoking videos.

Because you can piece together multiple shots (by stopping and starting your recording), Vine videos can be somewhat sophisticated in terms of look and story. Vine's start/stop recording also enables you to create stop-motion videos, where each short shot functions as a single frame in the continuous movie.

Most people, however, use Vine to share what they're doing with their friends. You can opt to "follow" your friends on Vine, so that all the new videos they post automatically appear on your Vine home screen. Likewise, anyone following you will see your latest videos on their home screens. This is social networking, like you do with Facebook and Twitter, but with short videos instead of text-based messages.

In this fashion, you can keep abreast of what your friends are up to, and they'll know what you're doing, too. You might even make new friends who discover your videos on Vine and like what they see.

Summary

In this lesson, you learned what Vine is and what you can do with it. You also learned about the Vine app for iOS and Android devices, and about sharing your Vine videos via social networking.

LESSON 2

Downloading and Signing Up for Vine

In this lesson, you learn how to find and download the Vine app for your mobile device, and how to sign up for a new Vine account.

Downloading the Vine App for iOS Devices

The Vine app is available for both iOS and Android devices. On the iOS platform, you can install and use the Vine app on iPhones, iPad tablets, and iPod touch wireless music players. All these devices have built-in cameras for shooting videos.

Whichever Apple device you're using, you download the Vine app (free) from the App Store. Follow these steps:

1. From your device's home screen, tap the App Store icon.

2. When the App Store opens, tap Search at the bottom of the screen.

3. Enter [**vine**] into the search box at the top of the screen, as shown in Figure 2.1, then tap Search.

4. When the search results appear, as shown in Figure 2.2, scroll to the Vine app and tap the Install button.

5. You're now warned that Vine contains age-restricted material. Click OK to continue.

FIGURE 2.1   Searching for the Vine app in Apple's App Store.

FIGURE 2.2   Downloading and installing the Vine app on an iPhone.

The App Store now installs the Vine app and displays an icon for the app on the first free screen on your device.

Downloading the Vine App for Android Devices

The Vine app is also available for Android phones and tablets, from the Google Play online store. Like the iOS version, Vine's Android app is completely free.

Follow these steps to download and install the Vine app on your Android device:

1. From your device's home screen, tap the Play Store icon.

2. When the Google Play Store opens, tap Apps.

3. Tap the Search icon at the top of the screen to display the search box.

4. Enter [vine] into the search box, then tap Search.

5. When the search results appear, scroll to and tap the Vine app.

6. From the details screen, tap the Install button.

7. When prompted, tap Accept & Download to begin downloading the app.

The Vine app is now downloaded to and installed on your Android device.

Signing Up for a New Vine Account

The first time you launch the Vine app on your mobile device, you're prompted to either sign in with an existing account or create a new account. You can sign up to Vine using your existing Twitter account, if you have one, or you can create a completely new account based on your email address.

> NOTE: **Use Your Current Location**
>
> The first time you launch the Vine app you're informed that Vine would like to use your current location. Click OK to enable Vine to automatically add location information to your video posts.

Signing In with Twitter

If you have a Twitter account, the easiest way to sign into Vine is with that account. In fact, if you're currently logged into Twitter on your mobile device, Vine will automatically use your Twitter account information to create a new Vine account, and open the app directly into that new account.

> NOTE: **Twitter Info**
>
> When you sign into Vine using your Twitter account, your Vine account will include all the profile information—and profile picture—you previously supplied to Twitter. You will be able to edit some of this information later, as detailed in Lesson 4, "Personalizing Vine."

If the Vine app does not automatically sign in with your Twitter account info, you can do this manually. Follow these steps:

1. From your mobile device, tap the Vine icon to launch the Vine app, as shown in Figure 2.3.

2. Tap Sign In with Twitter, as shown in Figure 2.4.

3. If you have the Twitter app installed on your device, the Vine app will automatically sign into Vine using your Twitter account name and password; you don't have to manually enter any information.

4. If the Twitter app is not installed on your device, tap Sign In with Twitter.

5. Enter your Twitter handle and password as requested.

FIGURE 2.3   Tap the Vine icon to launch the Vine app.

FIGURE 2.4   Signing into Vine with your Twitter account.

Signing Up with an Email Address

If you don't have a Twitter account, or don't want to link your Vine and Twitter accounts, you can instead create a new Vine account based on your email address. Follow these steps:

1. From your mobile device, tap the Vine icon to launch the Vine app.

2. Tap Sign Up with Email.

3. From the first Sign Up screen, shown in Figure 2.5, enter your full first and last name, then tap Next.

FIGURE 2.5   Creating a new Vine account.

4. When prompted to set up a profile photo, tap Skip. (You can do this later.)

5. When the next screen appears, as shown in Figure 2.6, enter your email address into the Email field.

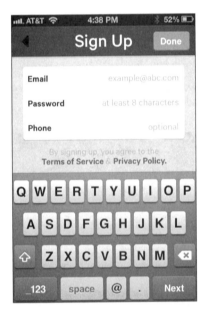

FIGURE 2.6   Manually entering information for your new Vine account.

6. Enter your desired password (eight characters minimum) into the Password field.

7. If you want (it's optional), enter your phone number into the Phone field.

8. Tap Done.

Vine now creates your new account and opens the Vine app for your use.

Signing In Manually

Vine should automatically log into your account whenever you tap the Vine icon to launch the Vine app—unless you've manually logged out of the app (as described in the following lesson). In this instance, you will need to manually sign in the next time you launch the app. Follow these steps:

1. From your mobile device, tap the Vine icon to launch the Vine app.

2. When prompted, tap Sign In Now.

3. When the next screen appears, as shown in Figure 2.7, enter your email address into the Email field.

FIGURE 2.7   Manually signing into your Vine account.

4. Enter your password into the Password field.

5. Tap Sign In.

Logging Out of Vine

By default, you stay logged into your Vine account, even when you close the Vine app. This means that the next time you open the Vine app, you should be automatically logged into your account.

You can, however, manually log out of your Vine account. This is useful if you have multiple people using Vine on a single mobile device. Follow these steps:

1. From within the Vine app, tap the Home icon to display the menu of options shown in Figure 2.8.

FIGURE 2.8   Tap Home > Profile to log off.

2. From your Profile screen, tap the Settings button.

3. Scroll to the bottom of the Settings screen and tap the Log Out button, shown in Figure 2.9.

You're now logged out of your Vine account. The next time you launch the Vine app, you'll have to log back into your account.

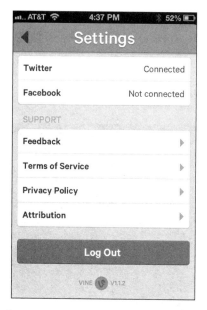

FIGURE 2.9   Logging out of your Vine account.

Summary

In this lesson, you learned how to download the Vine app from the Apple App Store or Google Play Store. You also learned how to create a new Vine account and sign into (and log out of) that account.

LESSON 3

Navigating Vine

In this lesson, you learn how to move around the Vine app.

Switching Screens

The Vine app is comprised of multiple screens, each with its own distinct functionality. You access each of these screens by tapping the Menu button that appears in the top-left corner of every screen. When you tap the Menu button you see the following choices, as shown in Figure 3.1:

FIGURE 3.1 Vine's Menu button and options.

▶ **Home.** Tap this option to return to the Home screen from any other screen.

- ▶ **Explore.** Tap this option to find vines to watch, either by browsing or searching.

- ▶ **Activity.** Tap this option to view likes and comments for and about the videos you've posted.

- ▶ **Profile.** Tap this option to view your Vine profile and edit your personal settings—as well as find other Vine users to follow.

Tap the menu button from any screen to change screens in the Vine app.

Exploring Vine's Screens

What's where in the Vine app? Each screen has its own unique functionality.

Exploring the Home Screen

The Home screen is what you see when you first launch the Vine app. As you can see in Figure 3.2, the Home screen contains a feed of videos from people you follow, as well as your own videos and Vine's Editor's Picks. The most recent videos appear first; scroll down to view older videos.

Vine videos play automatically when they are scrolled to on the Home screen. When you scroll down the screen to the next video, the previous video stops playing and the next video begins playing. Each video plays in a continuous loop until you either move to the next video or navigate to a different screen.

Beneath each video is a link to people who've liked this video, as well as comments on the video. You'll also find buttons for liking and making your own comments on the video.

NOTE: **Viewing Vines**

Learn more about watching Vine videos in Lesson 6, "Watching Vines."

FIGURE 3.2   Vine's Home screen—a feed of the most recent videos.

Exploring the Explore Screen

You use Vine's Explore screen to explore videos from other people. As you can see in Figure 3.3, there are a number of ways to find new videos on the Explore screen:

▶ Search for videos from the top-of-screen search box. You can search for people or for tags (keywords) that describe a video.

▶ View the most popular videos on the Vine site—what Vine calls Popular Now.

▶ View trending videos—what Vine calls On The Rise.

▶ Browse videos by category—Comedy, Art & Experimental, Cats, Dogs, Family, Beauty & Fashion, Food, Health & Fitness, Nature, Music, News & Politics, Special FX, Sports, Urban, and Weird.

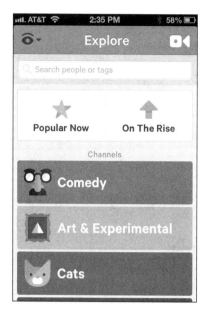

FIGURE 3.3   Finding new videos on Vine's Explore screen.

▶ Browse videos by trending hashtags—that is, videos that are increasing in popularity at the moment, based on other users searching for particular hashtags.

NOTE: **Finding Vines**

Learn more about browsing and searching for Vine videos in Lesson 5, "Finding Vines."

Exploring the Activity Screen

Want to see who's commenting on or liking the videos you've posted? Then turn to Vine's Activity screen, shown in Figure 3.4, where you can view the most recent likes and comments from viewers.

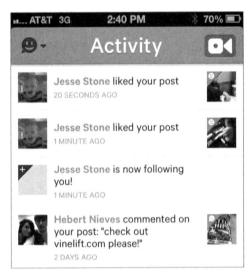

FIGURE 3.4 Viewing likes and comments on the Activity screen.

Exploring the Profile Screen

How do you look to other users? Open your Profile screen to find out. As you can see in Figure 3.5, your Profile screen contains your profile picture, a short description of yourself, where you live, and tabs to see the posts you've made and videos you've liked. There's also a Settings button to access your personal settings, and a Find People button (at the top) to find other users to follow.

Exploring the Settings Screen

When you tap the Settings button on your Profile screen, you open your Settings screen, shown in Figure 3.6. Here you can see and edit any of your account settings, including your contact information, preferences, and social networking connections.

NOTE: **Settings**
Learn more about configuring Vine's settings in Lesson 4, "Personalizing Vine."

FIGURE 3.5   Viewing your Vine profile.

FIGURE 3.6   Viewing and editing your account settings.

Exploring the Find People Screen

Tap the button at the top right of your Profile screen and you open Vine's Find People screen, shown in Figure 3.7. From here you can identify other Vine users to follow, on Twitter, from your own address book, or by searching for them.

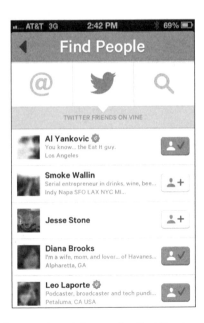

FIGURE 3.7   Finding people to follow on the Find People screen.

NOTE: **Finding People to Follow**
Learn more about finding and following other users in Lesson 7, "Following Other Vinesters."

Discovering the Shooting Screen

When you want to shoot a new Vine video, all you have to do is tap the Camera button at the top right of Vine's Home, Explore, or Activity screens. (This button does not appear on the Profile screen.) This displays the Shooting screen; as you can see in Figure 3.8, this is essentially a live picture from your smartphone or tablet camera. Tap and hold the screen to shoot. Release your finger to stop shooting. Tap the X at the top right to end your shooting session and return to the previous screen.

FIGURE 3.8   Shooting a new Vine video.

NOTE: **Settings**
Learn more about shooting Vine videos in Lesson 8, "Shooting a Vine."

Summary

In this lesson, you learned how to navigate the Vine app.

LESSON 4

Personalizing Vine

In this lesson, you learn how to personalize your Vine profile and configure important settings in the Vine app.

Customizing Your Vine Profile

If you signed into Vine with your Twitter credentials, Vine automatically imports information from your Twitter account to create your Vine profile. You can view your profile by tapping the Menu button and then tapping Profile.

Once you're on your Profile page, you can edit much of your profile information. This way, you can maintain a slightly different profile on Vine than you do on Twitter.

Change Your Profile Picture

The first thing you personalize about your Vine account is your profile picture. By default, Vine uses the same picture you use for your Twitter profile. You can select or take a different photo, however. Follow these steps:

1. Tap Menu > Profile to display your profile page, shown in Figure 4.1.

2. Tap your profile picture to show the available actions, as shown in Figure 4.2.

3. To remove the current photo without replacing it with a new one, tap Remove Photo.

FIGURE 4.1   Tap your profile picture to change it.

FIGURE 4.2   Remove your profile picture or choose a new one.

4. To upload a new photo stored on your phone or tablet, tap Choose Existing Photo. When your Camera Roll appears, tap the photo you want to use. When the Move and Scale screen appears, drag or resize the photo as necessary, then tap Choose.

5. To take a new photo with your phone's camera, tap Take New Photo. When your camera activates, tap to use the front-facing camera, smile, and tap the Camera button. When the Move and Scale screen appears, drag or resize the photo as necessary, then tap Use.

Change Your Name, Description, and Location

As noted, Vine pulls your name and other personal information from your Twitter account. If you want to change or correct this information for your Vine profile, you can. Follow these steps:

1. Tap Menu > Profile to display your profile page.

2. Tap Settings to display the Settings page, shown in Figure 4.3.

FIGURE 4.3　Editing your personal information.

3. To change the name displayed with your Vine posts, tap your name and edit it with the onscreen keyboard.

4. To change your description/occupation, tap it and then edit it with the onscreen keyboard.

5. To change your current location, tap it and then edit it with the onscreen keyboard.

Configuring Vine Settings

There are a handful of system settings for the Vine app that you might want or need to configure at some point. They're all accessible from the Settings page.

Enter or Change Contact Information

Vine would like to know how to contact you, via either email or phone. You don't have to enter either piece of information, but if you want to, you can. Follow these steps:

1. Tap Menu > Profile to display your profile page.

2. Tap Settings to display the Settings page.

3. Scroll to the Account section, shown in Figure 4.4.

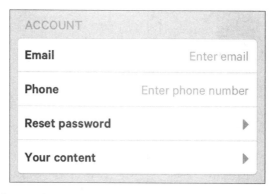

FIGURE 4.4   Editing your contact information.

4. To enter or change your email address, tap the Email field and edit it with the onscreen keyboard.

5. To enter or change your phone number, tap the Phone field and edit it with the onscreen keyboard.

Change Your Password

You should periodically change your account password to make it harder for identity thieves to hack into your Vine account. Follow these steps:

1. Tap Menu > Profile to display your profile page.

2. Tap Settings to display the Settings page.

3. Scroll to the Account section and tap Reset Password.

4. When prompted that instructions will be sent to your email address, tap Send.

5. Vine sends instructions for resetting the password to you via email. Follow these instructions to reset your password.

NOTE: **Reset via Email**

Vine requires you to have entered an email address before you can reset your system password. The reset instructions are sent to you via email, to keep hackers from changing your password without your knowledge.

Protect Your Posts

By default, everyone on Vine can see the videos you upload. You can, however, limit your viewership only to those people who are following you. This is called "protecting" your posts.

To protect your posts in this fashion, follow these steps:

1. Tap Menu > Profile to display your profile page.

2. Tap Settings to display the Settings page.

3. Scroll to the Account section and tap Your Content to display the Your Content page, shown in Figure 4.5.

4. Tap "on" the Posts Are Protected switch.

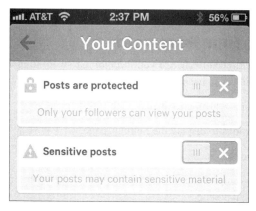

FIGURE 4.5   Configuring Vine content options.

> NOTE: **Make Public**
> You can switch "off" the Posts Are Protected option at any time to make your posts public again.

Post Sensitive Material

If you think your vines are going to contain material that may be offensive to some viewers, you may want to flag them as such. Follow these steps to tell people your account may contain sensitive material:

1. Tap Menu > Profile to display your profile page.

2. Tap Settings to display the Settings page.

3. Scroll to the Account section and tap Your Content to display the Your Content page.

4. Tap "on" the Sensitive Posts switch.

> NOTE: **Disable Sensitive Posts**
>
> If you find your posts *don't* contain offensive material, you can switch "off" the Sensitive Posts option at any time.

Connect to Your Twitter and Facebook Accounts

By default, your Vine account is connected to your Twitter account. If you've entered an email address into your contact information, you can disconnect these accounts if you like. In addition, you can connect your Vine account to your Facebook account, so that the videos you post to Vine are cross-posted to Facebook.

Follow these steps:

1. Tap Menu > Profile to display your profile page.

2. Tap Settings to display the Settings page.

3. Scroll to the Social Networks section, shown in Figure 4.6.

FIGURE 4.6 Connecting to your Twitter and Facebook accounts.

4. To disconnect your Twitter account, tap Twitter. When the next panel appears, tap Disconnect Twitter.

5. To connect your Facebook account, tap Facebook. If you're currently logged into Facebook on your mobile device, Vine will connect your accounts automatically. If not, you'll be prompted to enter your Facebook username and password.

Summary

In this lesson, you learned how to enter and edit personal information in your Vine profile, and to configure important Vine settings.

Finding Vines

In this lesson, you learn several different ways to find interesting Vine videos to watch.

Exploring Popular and Trending Videos

Vine hosts millions of individual videos—which means you should be able to find a few interesting ones to watch. Fortunately, Vine offers several different ways to discover new videos.

Viewing Popular Videos

Want to see which videos are popular among other Vinesters? Then check out Vine's Popular Now videos. There's a reason these videos are the most watched; they're either extremely entertaining or about topics that are gathering a lot of interest.

1. Tap the Menu button and select Explore to display the Explore page, shown in Figure 5.1.

2. Tap Popular Now to display the Popular Now page.

3. Scroll down to view all popular videos.

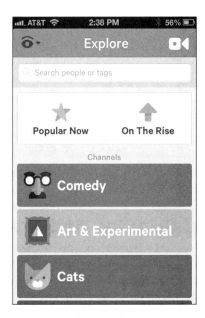

FIGURE 5.1   Explore new vines from the Explore page.

Viewing On The Rise Videos

It may also be worth your while to explore videos that are "on the rise"—
that is, are trending upwards in popularity. Follow these steps:

1. Tap the Menu button and select Explore to display the Explore
   page.

2. Tap On The Rise to display the On The Rise page.

3. Scroll down to view all trending videos.

Viewing Vines by Channel

Vine has organized all of its user videos into a handful of popular cate-
gories, which it calls *channels*. These channels include the following:

▶ Comedy	▶ Nature
▶ Art & Experimental	▶ Music
▶ Cats	▶ News & Politics
▶ Dogs	▶ Special FX
▶ Family	▶ Sports
▶ Beauty & Fashion	▶ Urban
▶ Food	▶ Weird
▶ Health & Science	

To view videos in a given channel, follow these steps:

1. Tap the Menu button and select Explore to display the Explore page.

2. Scroll to the Channels section to view available channels.

3. Tap a channel to view the page for that channel, as shown in Figure 5.2.

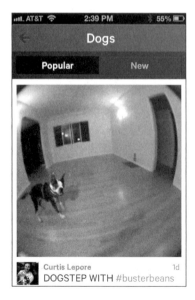

FIGURE 5.2 Viewing vines in a specific channel.

4. Tap the Popular tab to view the most popular vines in this category.

5. Tap the New tab to view the newest vines in this category.

Using Hashtags to Find New Videos

A *hashtag* is a word or phrase, preceded by the hash symbol (#), that identifies important content in Vine video. Think of a hashtag as a keyword. When someone posts a Vine video, she adds one or more hashtags to call out the content of the video. You can then search for specific hashtags to find videos that contain that specific content.

NOTE: **Hashtags**

Hashtags originated on Twitter as a means of embedding keywords in messages. Identifying a keyword with a hash symbol makes it easier to search for specific content.

For example, if someone shoots a vine at a local basketball game, he might tag that video with **#basketball**. If you search Vine for the **#basketball** hashtag, you'll find that video—as well as any other videos identified with that hashtag.

NOTE: **Not Case Sensitive**

Hashtags are *not* case sensitive, so **#basketball** is the same as **#Basketball** or **#BASKETBALL**. A hashtag can contain one or more words, but without spaces between the words. So, for example, a video about high school basketball could be tagged with **#highschoolbasketball**.

Viewing Trending Hashtags

What are the hottest hashtags today? Check out Vine's *trending* hashtags, those that are gaining the most momentum on the service—that is, those are moving up the most in popularity, not necessarily those with the most posts. Follow these steps:

1. Tap the Menu button and select Explore to display the Explore page.

2. Scroll down the page to the Trending Tags section to view Vine's trending hashtags, as shown in Figure 5.3.

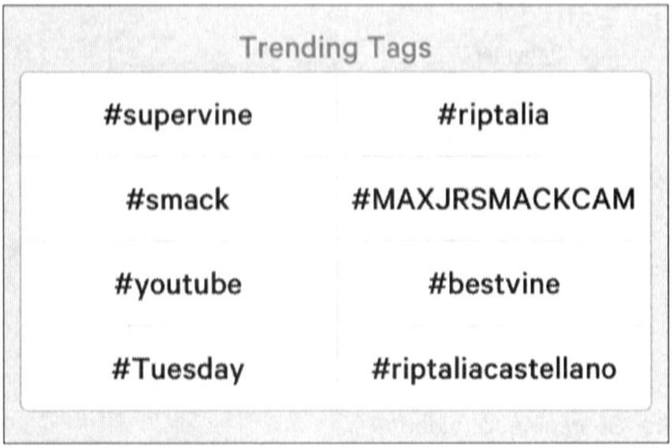

Trending Tags	
#supervine	#riptalia
#smack	#MAXJRSMACKCAM
#youtube	#bestvine
#Tuesday	#riptaliacastellano

FIGURE 5.3   View vines tagged with hashtags that are gaining in popularity.

3. Tap the icon for a particular hashtag to view all recent videos tagged with that hashtag.

Searching for Hashtags

You can also search Vine for videos tagged with a specific hashtag. Follow these steps to search for hashtags:

1. Tap the Menu button and select Explore to display the Explore page.

2. Enter a keyword into the Search box at the top of the page. You do *not* have to enter the # symbol before the keyword.

3. When the two tabs appear, as shown in Figure 5.4, tap the Tags tab.

FIGURE 5.4   Searching for videos.

4. As you type, Vine displays a list of suggested hashtags. Tap the hashtag you'd like to view.

5. Vine displays a page of videos that contain the desired hashtag. Scroll down the page to view more tagged videos.

TIP: **Web Searching**

There are several sites, such as VineViewer, VineRoulette, and Seenive, that let you search for Vine videos from any web browser. Learn more in Lesson 19, "Viewing Vines on Other Sites."

Searching for People on Vine

You can also search Vine for specific people, and then view the videos they've posted. Follow these steps to search for people on Vine:

1. Tap the Menu button and select Explore to display the Explore page.

2. Enter all or part of the person's username into the Search box at the top of the page.

3. When the two tabs appear, as shown in Figure 5.5, tap the People tab.

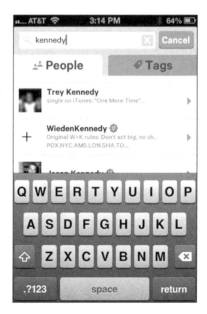

FIGURE 5.5 Searching for people.

4. As you type, Vine displays a list of suggested users. Tap the user you'd like to view.

5. Vine displays that person's profile page. Tap the Posts tab to view that person's videos.

Summary

In this lesson, you learned how to find new Vine videos by browsing Popular and On The Rise videos, browsing by category-specific channel, and by searching for specific hashtags. You also learned to search for Vine videos posted by specific people.

Watching Vines

In this lesson, you discover how to view Vine videos on your smartphone or tablet, and on the Web from Twitter and Facebook.

Viewing a Vine on Your Mobile Device

Most Vinesters watch vines on their smartphones and tablets. After all, Vine was designed with mobile devices in mind. To that end, you use the Vine app to watch your favorite vines.

Watching a Vine

In most instances, viewing a vine is as easy as navigating to it; playback starts automatically. Follow these steps:

1. Navigate to the video you want to view and position it in the center of your device's screen, as shown in Figure 6.1.

2. Playback should start automatically and continue looping back to the beginning, over and over again.

3. To pause playback, tap the screen. Tap the screen again to resume playback.

4. To play another video, scroll down the page or otherwise navigate to that video. Playback of the first video will stop when it moves from the center of the screen; playback of the second video will begin when it is positioned in the center of the screen.

FIGURE 6.1   Playing a vine.

> TIP: **Adjusting the Volume**
> You can't adjust or mute the sound level of a video from within the Vine app. Use your phone or tablet's volume controls to raise or lower the playback volume, or turn off your device's sound to mute the playback.

Liking a Vine

If you come across a vine that you find particularly interesting, you can "like" that vine. It's the equivalent of giving the vine a big thumbs up. Follow these steps:

1. Navigate to the particular video.

2. Tap the smiley face icon, shown in Figure 6.2, to like the video.

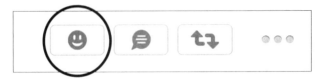

FIGURE 6.2   Tap the smiley face icon to like the video.

TIP: **Change Your Mind**
If you change your mind about a video, or just accidentally tap the Like icon, tap the icon again to "unlike" the video.

Commenting on a Vine

You can comment on a vine, just as you can a post on Facebook or a tweet on Twitter. Other viewers' comments are listed beneath the video itself. Follow these steps to add your comments:

1. Navigate to the particular video.

2. Tap the Comments icon to display the "Say something nice" comments box, shown in Figure 6.3.

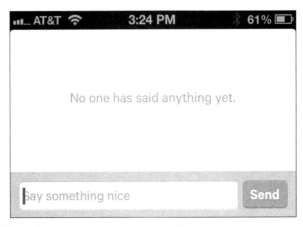

FIGURE 6.3   Entering comments about a video.

3. Use the onscreen keyboard to type your comments.

4. To reference another user in your comments, tap the "person" icon to add the @ symbol in the comments box, then enter that person's Vine username.

5. To include a hashtag in your comments, tap the "tag" icon to add the # symbol in the comments box, then type the hashtag.

6. Tap the Send button to add your comments.

TIP: **Deleting a Comment**

If you post a comment in error, or that later you regret, you can delete that comment. Go to the post in question and tap the Comments icon to display the Comments page. Go to your comment and swipe it from the right to the left to display the big red X. Tap the X to delete the comment.

TIP: **Reporting a Vine**

If you find a vine that's offensive to you, for whatever reason, you can report that video to Vine's powers that be. Tap the More (three dot) icon beneath the video, then tap the Report This Post button.

Viewing the Poster's Profile

To find out more about the person behind the post, you can tap through to view any poster's Vine profile. Follow these steps:

1. Navigate to the particular video.

2. Tap the poster's name, located just beneath the video and above the accompanying text, to display this person's Vine profile page.

Viewing a Vine on Your Computer

Vine was conceived as a video-sharing service for mobile devices. However, because you can share vines via Twitter and Facebook, you can also view those vines on any personal computer.

> NOTE: **Sharing a Vine**
>
> To learn more about sharing vines via Twitter and Facebook, as well as "revining" videos to your Vine followers, see Lesson 11, "Sharing Your Vine."

Viewing a Vine from a Tweet

When someone shares a vine via Twitter, a link to that vine appears in that person's tweet. To view the vine, follow these steps:

1. From your Twitter feed, navigate to the tweet that contains the link to the Vine video, as shown in Figure 6.4.

FIGURE 6.4   A vine linked to from a tweet.

2. Click the View Media link to display the video within your Twitter feed, as shown in Figure 6.5.

3. To begin playback, click the video.

4. Playback will continue as the video loops back to the beginning. To pause playback, click the video again.

5. By default, audio is muted on playback. To listen to the sound, click the speaker icon in the top-left corner of the video.

6. To view the video on its own web page, as shown in Figure 6.6, click the View On Web link.

FIGURE 6.5   Playing a vine within your Twitter feed.

FIGURE 6.6   Playing a vine on its own web page.

7. Playback begins automatically. To pause playback, click the
   video.

8. To listen to the video's sound, click the speaker icon in the
   top-left corner of the video.

Viewing a Vine from Facebook

When someone shares a vine via Facebook, a link to that vine appears in
that person's Facebook status update, along with a thumbnail image from
the video. To view the vine, follow these steps:

1. From your Facebook News feed, navigate to the status update
   that contains the link to the Vine video, as shown in Figure 6.7.

FIGURE 6.7   A vine in a Facebook status update.

2. Click the link to the vine (or the thumbnail image) to display the
   vine's web page, as shown in Figure 6.8.

3. Playback begins automatically. To pause playback, click the
   video. Click the video again to resume playback.

4. By default, the sound for the video is muted. To listen to the
   video, click the speaker icon in the top-left corner.

Michael Miller

Organ music.

MADE WITH 𝒱𝒾𝓃𝑒

Download App

FIGURE 6.8   Playing a vine.

Summary

In this lesson, you learned how to watch Vine videos, as well as how to like and comment on them. You also learned how to view vines on your computer from both Twitter and Facebook.

LESSON 7

Following Other Vinesters

In this lesson, you learn how to find other Vine users and follow their latest videos.

Finding Other Vinesters

Vine has millions of users, some of whom you might know or be interested in. How do you find other people on Vine? There are a number of ways.

Finding Twitter Friends

Chances are that many of the people you follow on Twitter are also on Vine. The Vine app makes it easy to find and follow Twitter friends. Follow these steps:

1. Tap the Menu button and select Profile to display your Profile page, shown in Figure 7.1.

2. Tap the People button at the top-right corner to display the Find People page, shown in Figure 7.2.

3. Tap the Twitter button to display a list of your Twitter friends who are on Vine.

4. Tap a friend's name to display her profile page.

5. Tap the Add button to follow that friend on your Vine Home page.

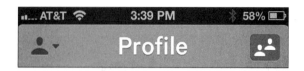

FIGURE 7.1   Tap the People button to display the Find People page.

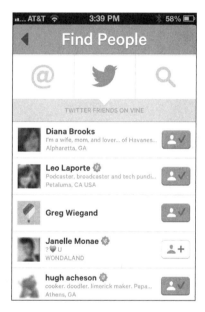

FIGURE 7.2   Finding your Twitter friends on Vine.

Finding Friends From Your Address Book

Vine can also search your mobile device's address book to find contacts who are also on Vine. Follow these steps:

1. Tap the Menu button and select Profile to display your Profile page.

2. Tap the People button at the top-right corner to display the Find People page.

3. Tap the Address Book (@) button, shown in Figure 7.3.

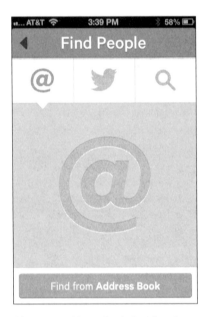

FIGURE 7.3   Searching your address book for Vinesters.

4. Tap Find from Address Book to display a list of your contacts who are on Vine.

5. Tap a contact's name to display her profile page.

6. Tap the Add button to follow that person on your Vine Home page.

Searching for People

Maybe you're looking for a particular person who you know or think is using Vine. Vine lets you search its user base to find specific people. Follow these steps:

1. Tap the Menu button and select Profile to display your Profile page.

2. Tap the People button at the top-right corner to display the Find People page.

3. Tap the Search (magnifying glass) button, shown in Figure 7.4.

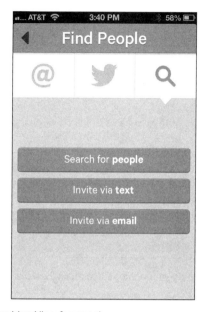

FIGURE 7.4   Searching Vine for people.

4. Tap the Search for People button to display the search page.

5. Enter the person's name into the search box.

6. As you type, suggested users are listed beneath the search box. Tap a name to display a person's profile page.

7. Tap the Add button to follow a specific person.

Searching From the Search Box

You can also search Vine from the search box found at the top of the Explore page. Follow these steps:

1. Tap the Menu button and select Explore to display the Explore page.

2. Tap within the search box to display the People and Tags tabs, shown in Figure 7.5.

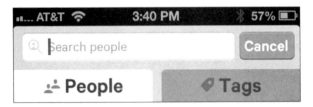

FIGURE 7.5   Using the Explore page search box.

3. Tap the People tab.

4. Enter the person's name into the search box.

5. As you type, suggested users are listed beneath the search box. Tap a name to display a person's profile page.

6. Tap the Follow button to follow a specific person.

Inviting a Friend via Text Message

What do you do if a person you know isn't on Vine yet? You can invite him to join up, and then choose to follow him. Here's how to invite a person via text message:

1. Tap the Menu button and select Profile to display your Profile page.

2. Tap the People button at the top-right corner to display the Find People page.

3. Tap the Search (magnifying glass) button.

4. Tap the Invite via Text button to display the New Message page, shown in Figure 7.6. A message from Vine is already entered, including a link to join Vine.

FIGURE 7.6   Sending a text invite.

5. Enter your friend's mobile phone number into the To: field.

6. Press the Send button to send the message.

When your friend receives the text message, he can click the link to connect to Vine and create a new account.

Inviting a Friend via Email

You can also invite friends via traditional email. Follow these steps:

1. Tap the Menu button and select Profile to display your Profile page.

2. Tap the People button at the top-right corner to display the Find People page.

3. Tap the Search (magnifying glass) button.

4. Tap the Invite via Email button to display a new email message, shown in Figure 7.7. A message from Vine is already entered, including a link to join Vine.

5. Enter your friend's email address into the To: field.

6. Tap the Send button to send the email.

FIGURE 7.7 Sending an email invite.

When your friend opens the email message, he can click the link to connect to Vine and create a new account.

Viewing Profile Pages

Every Vine user has his own personal profile page. You can choose to follow a person from this page, as well as learn more about that individual.

To view a person's profile page, simply click his name anywhere on the Vine site. This displays the screen shown in Figure 7.8. You see the person's profile picture at the top of the screen, with an optional short bio/description underneath. Then there's a Follow button, which you tap to (naturally) follow that person. Beneath that are two tabs, one for Posts (videos this person has posted) and one for Likes (other people's videos this person has liked). Scroll down to view more videos.

FIGURE 7.8   Viewing a user's Vine profile page.

Tap the More button at the top-right to see three more options. You can
Block This Person (keep this person from viewing your videos), Report
This Person (if this person is harassing you), or Share This Profile (via
text message with a friend).

Following People

When you want to see all of a person's new videos on your Home screen,
you need to *follow* that person. Following a person is a one-way activity;
you see all of her videos, but she doesn't necessarily see all of yours—
unless she decides to follow you as well.

After you've followed a person, all of that person's videos are displayed
on your Vine Home screen. Any time this person posts a new video, it
shows up on your Home screen.

Choosing to Follow

The easiest way to follow a person is from that individual's profile page. Follow these steps:

1. Tap the person's name anywhere on the Vine site to display his profile page.

2. Tap the Follow button.

Unfollowing a Person

You might find that some of the people you follow aren't worth following. Maybe they don't post enough videos, or maybe they post too many—or too many that you're not that interested in. You can, at any time, choose to unfollow a person. Follow these steps:

1. Tap the person's name anywhere on the Vine site to display his profile page.

2. Tap the Following button.

The Following button now changes to a Follow button, which means you're no longer following this person.

View—and Manage—the People You Follow

You can, at any time, view the list of Vinesters you're following—and remove them from your list of followers. Follow these steps:

1. Tap Home > Profile to display your own profile page.

2. View the number of people you are following beneath your name and bio, as shown in Figure 7.9.

3. Tap *X* **Following** to display the Following page, shown in Figure 7.10, with all the people you follow listed.

4. Tap the green checked box next to a person's name to unfollow that person.

FIGURE 7.9   Go to your own profile page to see how many people you're following, and who are following you.

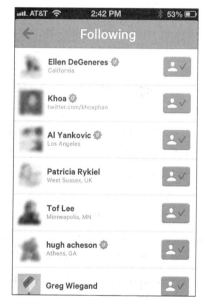

FIGURE 7.10   Viewing the people you're following.

View Your Followers

Want to know who's following you on Vine? Here's how:

1. Tap Home > Profile to display your own profile page.

2. View the number of people who have followed you beneath your name and bio.

3. Tap *X* **Follower(s)** to display the Followers page, with all your followers listed.

Summary

In this lesson, you learned how to find people on Vine, and how to follow their videos.

LESSON 8

Shooting a Vine

In this lesson, you learn how to record and upload short Vine videos.

Basic Recording

Shooting a six-second video doesn't sound all that difficult, but there are some basic operations that everyone needs to know.

Shooting a Continuous Video

Recording a Vine video is pretty much a point-and-shoot operation. That is, you point your phone's camera at whatever it is you want to record, and then tap the screen to begin shooting.

Follow these steps to record a basic video:

1. Tap the camera button at the top-right of the Home, Explore, or Activity screens, as shown in Figure 8.1.

FIGURE 8.1   Tap the camera button to begin recording.

2. Point your camera's phone at your subject.

CAUTION: **Vertical, Not Horizontal**

Vine videos are essentially square, and designed to be viewed when holding a mobile phone vertically in your hand. Do *not* shoot a vine with your phone turned horizontally, or it will display sideways when others view it.

---

3. Tap and hold the screen to begin recording. The green progress bar above the recording area displays how long you've been recording, as shown in Figure 8.2.

FIGURE 8.2   Recording a Vine video.

4. Raise your finger from the screen to halt recording.

TIP: **Three-Second Minimum**

Although Vine enables recordings up to six seconds in length, you don't have to record quite that long. Vine will consider a video complete if it's at least three seconds long. (The right arrow button appears after you've reached the three-second mark.)

---

5. If you record less than six seconds, tap the right arrow button to display the preview screen. Otherwise, the preview screen displays automatically when the maximum length is reached.

6. If you like what you see, tap the big green checkmark button to display the Share screen.

7. Use the onscreen keyboard to add a description of the video into the Add a Caption box, shown in Figure 8.3.

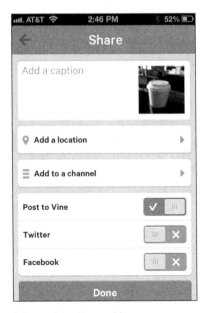

FIGURE 8.3 Describing and posting a video.

8. Tap the Add a Location box to display a list of nearby places. Tap a given location to select where the video was recorded, or use the search box to search for other locations.

9. Tap the Add To a Channel box to display a list of Vine channels. Tap a given channel to place your vine in this category.

10. Make sure the Post to Vine option is checked.

11. To also post this video to Twitter, check the Twitter option.

12. To also post this video to Facebook, check the Facebook option.

13. Tap the Done button.

NOTE: **Describing Your Video**

Learn more about captions, locations, and channels in Lesson 9, "Describing Your Vine."

NOTE: **Camera Roll**

Every Vine video you shoot automatically is saved as a video file in your mobile device's camera roll.

Shooting with the Front-Facing Camera

If your mobile device has a front-facing camera, you can opt to use it instead of the normal camera. This is good if you want to shoot a video of yourself, instead of someone else.

Follow these steps:

1. Tap the camera button at the top-right of the Home, Explore, or Activity screen.

2. Tap the Switch Camera button at the lower-left corner of the screen to switch to the front-facing camera, as shown in Figure 8.4.

FIGURE 8.4   Tap the Switch Camera button to switch to the front-facing camera.

3. Record and post your video as described previously.

TIP: **Zoom**

The Vine app for Android includes a nifty digital zoom feature that lets you zoom into the frame, making the subject larger. To zoom in, press and hold your phone's volume up button. To zoom back out, press and hold the volume down button. (This feature is slated to be added to the iPhone app in the near future.)

Displaying a Grid

To help position objects in a shot, Vine lets you superimpose a nine-cell grid over the viewing window. This grid is only for positioning purposes; it is not recorded in your final shot.

To display the grid while shooting, follow these steps:

1. Tap the camera button at the top-right of the Home, Explore, or Activity screen.

2. Tap the Grid button at the bottom of the shooting screen, shown in Figure 8.5.

3. Tap the button again to hide the grid.

FIGURE 8.5 Tap the Grid button to display a grid on the viewscreen.

Focusing on a Point in the Picture

Your phone or tablet camera doesn't always focus on what you want it to focus on. Vine corrects this problem by offering a "tap to focus" feature.

To use this feature to focus on a specific point in your picture, follow these steps:

1. Tap the camera button at the top-right of the Home, Explore, or Activity screen.

2. Tap the Focus button at the bottom of the shooting screen, as shown in Figure 8.6.

FIGURE 8.6   Tap the Focus button to activate the app's "tap to focus" feature.

3. Tap the point on your screen where you want the camera to focus.

4. Continue shooting your video as normal.

Creating a Video with Multiple Shots

A Vine video doesn't have to be a single continuous shot. You can record a video that has multiple shots, each as short as a fraction of a second. In this way you can use a vine to tell a story, or to offer step-by-step instruction.

Shooting Multiple Shots

Follow these steps to include multiple shots in a Vine video:

1. Tap the camera button at the top-right of the Home, Explore, or Activity screen.

2. Tap and hold the screen to begin recording.

3. Lift your finger to pause recording. The recording will remain paused until you tap the screen again; use this time to position your next shot.

4. Tap and hold the screen to resume recording.

5. Lift your finger to pause recording again.

6. Repeat steps 4 and 5 to record additional shots in this video.

7. When you're done recording, proceed to describe and post your video.

TIP: **Stop Motion**

You can also use Vine to shoot stop motion videos, one frame at a time. Just tap (and not hold) the screen to shoot a single frame, then repeat. Learn more in Lesson 15, "Creating a Stop Motion Video."

Showing a "Ghost" of a Previous Shot

When you're lining up multiple shots, one after another, it may be useful to see where the previous shot was positioned. Vine facilitates this by letting you display a "ghost" of the previous shot on top of the current shot. This is particularly useful when lining up shots for stop motion animation.

1. Shoot your first shot as normal.

2. Tap the Ghost button at the bottom of the screen. This displays a "ghost" image of the previous shot, as shown in Figure 8.7.

3. Use the ghost image to position your next shot. In stop motion animation, you would position the new shot almost on top of the previous one.

4. Tap the Ghost button again to hide the ghost image.

FIGURE 8.7   Tap the Ghost button to display a ghost image of the previous shot—and then use it to line up your next shot.

Deleting a Video

What do you do if you don't like a video you've shot? Vine lets you delete any video you've shot—even after you've posted it.

Deleting a Video

You can delete any video before you post it by following these steps:

1. Move to the preview screen and then tap the X at the top-right corner.

2. When prompted, tap the Delete Post button.

Deleting a Video After Posting

To delete a video *after* you've posted it, follow these steps:

1. Display the video and tap the More (three dots) button at the bottom-right of the screen.

2. When the next panel appears, tap the Delete Post button.

Tips for Advanced Recording

As you can see, basic Vine recording is fairly easy—just tap and release. That said, there are some more advanced techniques you can employ to record more sophisticated videos.

Watch the Light

The cameras built into most smartphones don't always have the best of lenses, which means they don't let in a lot of light. This results in grainy or dark pictures when you shoot in available room light or shade.

You can improve the look of your Vine videos by shooting in better lighting conditions. This might mean moving outside to take advantage of natural sunlight, turning on more lights if you're shooting inside, or even supplementing the available light with some sort of external lighting kit. The more light you have, the better looking your videos will be.

Keep the Camera Steady

Shaky, jerky videos are no fun to watch, and it's especially difficult to keep a small, lightweight phone steady while you're recording. Try holding the phone with two hands instead of one, or even bracing your elbows on a table or other solid surface.

TIP: **Use a Tripod**

An even better way to shoot a rock-solid video is to mount your camera phone on a tripod or monopod. Learn more about these and other useful accessories in Lesson 17, "Using Accessories for Better Vines."

Fade In

The abrupt start of a video can be a bit jarring, especially given Vine's looping playback. You can provide a more subtle start to your video by approximating a fade-in at the beginning.

You accomplish a fade-in effect by following these steps:

1. Place a sheet of cardboard, heavy paper, or just your hand in front of the camera lens for a few seconds. This tricks your phone's camera into thinking it's recording a dark scene.

2. When you're ready to record, remove the sheet of cardboard (or your hand) and then tap the screen to record. The camera now adjusts its iris for the current amount of light, which creates a fade in from total white to the scene you're recording.

TIP: **Fading Out**

Accomplishing a fade-out effect is similar but a bit more tricky. If you can *quickly* cover the camera lens with your hand or sheet of cardboard, the iris will adjust and fade the picture to white. The key is speed; you want to cover the lens without the camera seeing you do so.

Set the Lens Before You Record

Building on the preceding tip, if you don't want to fade into a video, you need to make sure your camera is properly set up before you start to record. Here's what you need to do:

1. Point your camera phone at the subject for a few seconds to let the iris adjust to the ambient lighting.

2. Adjust the focus (or use the Vine app's Focus button) to make sure the camera is focused correctly on the subject.

After everything is locked in, *then* you can tap the screen to start recording.

Use the Rule of Thirds

When it comes to framing your shots, the Rule of Thirds rules. This is a tried and tested photographic technique in which you divide the frame into thirds, both from side-to-side and from top-to-bottom.

You can use the Vine app's built-in Grid function to do this, as shown in Figure 8.8. For a more satisfying composition, position the subject at the intersection of any horizontal and vertical line—toward the side of the frame instead of directly in the middle.

FIGURE 8.8   Use the Rule of Thirds—and the Vine app's Grid function—to position the subject toward the right or left side of the frame.

Record From a Distance

You might want to include yourself in a video—which is difficult, as you have to be close to your phone to tap the screen to record. There's a trick you can use, however, to put some distance between yourself and your phone's screen:

1. Use duct tape to attach an AA or AAA battery to the end of a yardstick or similar long item. Make sure the positive end of the battery is facing out.

2. To begin recording, touch and hold the positive end of the battery to the phone's screen. This has the same effect as touching the screen with your finger.

3. Remove the battery from the screen to stop recording.

Pay Attention to the Sound

Remember, Vine records audio along with your video. Make sure that your subject is close enough to your camera phone to clearly capture what she's saying. And avoid situations where background noise might intrude into the video.

> TIP: **Use a Microphone**
> For the best possible sound, consider connecting an external micro-phone to your mobile phone, as discussed in Lesson 17.

Summary

In this lesson, you learned how to record and post Vine videos.

LESSON 9

Describing Your Vine

In this lesson, you learn how to write effective text descriptions for your Vine videos.

Why Descriptions Are Important

A Vine video is designed to capture the moment. As such, it stands on its own as a short video document of a place, a person, or a mood.

These moving images, however, need to be accompanied by descriptive text, words that tell people what they're going to see before they view it. And these words are every bit as important as the videos they accompany.

Here's why: When someone is searching for a new video to watch, she enters a search query. This works pretty much like a search on Google, Bing, or other web-based search engines. In the case of Vine, the words in the query are matched to the words in a video's description. In other words, when someone is searching Vine, she's searching the video descriptions, not the videos themselves. (There is no existing technology that enables the searching of still or moving images; all current searches are text searches.)

So if you want a video to be discoverable via search, you have to write a description that is optimized for searching. That is, your description has to both describe the video and include those keywords that people might be searching for.

Writing an Effective Caption

You enter the description of your Vine video into the Caption box on the Share screen that appears after you've shot the video. (See Lesson 8, "Shooting a Vine," for more details.)

What, exactly, should you write for your video's caption? Read on to garner some hints.

CAUTION: **No Edits**

Like Vine videos themselves, your videos' captions cannot be edited. If you don't like a caption you've added, there's no way to change it—short of deleting the entire video, that is.

Be Descriptive

The main purpose of your video's caption is to describe the content of the video. You need to tell whoever is searching for or browsing to a video what he should expect to see. Some people might only read the description and, on that basis, decide whether or not to view the video itself.

I like to view a vine description as a cross between a news headline and the first paragraph of a news story. Like a headline, the caption has to be descriptive, and pull people into watching the complete video. Like the first paragraph of a story, the caption has to tell a story, in summary form, and also pull people into further viewing.

So if a particular vine is a straightforward video of a baby laughing, your description should say just that. You might even include what the baby is laughing at, and end up with something like this:

Baby laughing at his dad's funny faces.

If a vine attempts to show how to cook a fried egg sandwich, write a description like this one:

How to cook a fried egg sandwich.

If a vine shows your girlfriend ordering lunch, say so:

My girlfriend ordering lunch.

Note that all of these captions are a single sentence in length. You can write more, but shouldn't write less. If you need a few sentences to describe your video, use them. If you can do it in one, that's great. But seldom can you describe your video in just a word or two; use complete sentences to create compelling captions.

NOTE: **Length**

Unlike the 140-character limit imposed by Vine's parent company, Twitter, there is no similar limit for your vine descriptions, so you can write as long a caption as you want. That doesn't mean you should compose an overly long description, however. It's a bit incongruent when you see a multiple-paragraph caption accompanying a six-second video. If you can tell your story in six seconds or less of video, you should be able to describe that video in a couple of sentences, max.

In fact, you can (and should) use the caption to elaborate on the main action, or to provide additional details. Take the video of your girlfriend ordering lunch, as an example. Where was she ordering? What's so interesting or unique about that? Here's where a longer caption might make sense, as follows:

My girlfriend ordering lunch at Burger King. She can't seem to figure out all the different options.

You can also use additional sentences to embellish the basic idea, as with the laughing baby video:

Our baby boy Benjamin laughing at his dad's funny faces. Have you ever heard a more infectious laugh?

You don't need to go much more in depth than that. A few sentences should be all you need to describe your video for anyone interested in watching it.

Write for Search

It's not only human beings who read the descriptions of your Vine videos. Vine's search engine analyzes the text of each caption to see whether it matches specific queries from users searching the Vine site.

As such, you need to write your descriptions with search engines in mind. That means including as many *keywords* as you can in your text. A keyword is simply a word or phrase that someone might search for; if your video's description includes the same keywords that a person is searching for, your video will show up in those particular search results. In other words, the better your write your descriptions, the more often your videos will be found.

For example, if your video demonstrates the perfect golf swing, **[golf]** and **[swing]** might be important keywords. You need to include these keywords in your video's text caption, like this:

Watch me demonstrate the perfect golf swing.

When someone is searching for **[golf]** or even **[golf swing]**, your video should then appear in those search results.

Likewise, if your vine documents your boyfriend snoring while sleeping, include the keywords **[sleeping]**, **[snoring]**, and **[boyfriend]**. If your video is of your new Nissan automobile, include the keywords **[car]**, **[automobile]**, and **[Nissan]**.

NOTE: **Not Case Sensitive**

Keywords are not case sensitive. You can write them as all uppercase, all lowercase, or initial caps.

The key is to think about how other people might be searching for this particular (or some similar) video. Use the words that other people will use in their queries. Those words become your keywords, and should be included in your video's caption.

Include Hashtags

Another way to optimize your video for search is to incorporate hashtags. A hashtag is a keyword or phrase preceded by the hash character (#). Users can search Vine for specific hashtags, as well as tap a hashtag in one description to display other videos that include the same hashtag.

Hashtags can be incorporated into the text of your caption, like this:

My #girlfriend likes #tacos.

Hashtags can also exist outside of the descriptive text, typically at the end of the caption, like this:

My girlfriend enjoying her lunch. #tacos #dietcoke

> NOTE: **Hashtags**
> Learn more about hashtags in Lesson 10, "Using Hashtags."

Tag Other Users

Vine also lets you mention or *tag* other users in your captions. A user who is tagged in a caption receives a notification on his Vine app's Activity screen, and his name is clickable (tappable) within the description. Tapping a tagged name opens that person's profile page.

To tag a user in a video caption, follow these steps:

1. Record your video as normal and proceed to the Share screen, shown in Figure 9.1.

2. Enter the @ sign, followed by the person's Vine username.

3. As you type, Vine displays a list of suggested users, as shown in Figure 9.2. Tap the correct name from the list, or continue typing the full name.

4. The tagged name now appears in your video's caption. Continue completing and posting the video as normal.

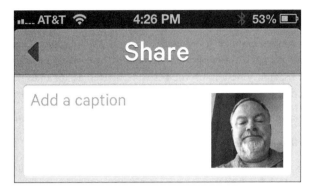

FIGURE 9.1   Composing the caption for a Vine video.

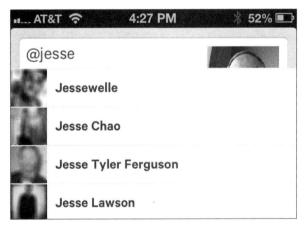

FIGURE 9.2   Tagging another user in a video caption.

Adding a Location to Your Vine

You can also tag your video with location information—typically, where you recorded the video. You add location info to your video from the Share screen, as follows:

1. Record your video as normal and proceed to the Share screen.

2. Tap Add a Location to display the Location screen, shown in Figure 9.3.

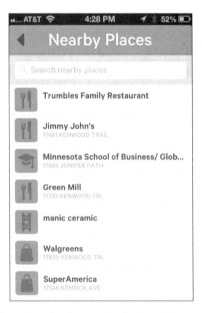

FIGURE 9.3 Adding a location to your vine's description.

3. Vine uses your phone's geolocation technology to suggest a list of nearby businesses and other locations. If your location is in this list, tap it to select it.

4. To enter a different location, enter the name of that place into the search box at the top of the screen.

5. Tap your location from the resulting list of search results. This location is added to your video's caption.

NOTE: **Foursquare**

Vine's location database is powered by Foursquare, a location-based social media service. Learn more at www.foursquare.com.

Summary

In this lesson, you learned how to write effective captions for your Vine videos.

LESSON 10

Using Hashtags

In this lesson, you learn how to use hashtags to enhance the discoverability of your videos.

Understanding Hashtags

A hashtag is a special type of keyword you can include in the descriptions for your Vine videos. It's essentially a keyword or phrase preceded by the hash (#) symbol.

Hashtags are clickable and searchable. When a viewer clicks on a hashtag in a video's description, Vine displays other videos tagged with that same hashtag. You can also search Vine by hashtag; the search results include other videos with that tag.

A hashtag starts with the # symbol followed by a single word, like this: **#car**. You can employ multiple words, but they have to run together; a hashtag cannot contain any spaces. So, for example, if you're describing a red car, you can use the hashtag **#redcar**, with no space between the two words.

> CAUTION: **Twitter Hashtags**
> The hash character identifies only the first word following. If you type the hashtag **#red car**, the hashtag registers just the first word, **#red**. The second word is not added as part of the hashtag.

Vine lets you use both upper- and lowercase characters in your hashtags. (Hashtags are not case sensitive.) You can also include numbers in your hashtags, but no other special characters, save for the # symbol.

When Vine encounters a special character in a hashtag, such as % or $, it ends the hashtag at that special character. So, for example, if you enter the hashtag **#bob'spresent**, the hashtag will be read as just **#bob**—everything after the special character is ignored.

Vine tracks the use of hashtags, and displays the most popular hashtags on the Explore screen. (Tap Menu > Explore to display.) Vine also displays trending hashtags, those that are being increasingly employed by users.

> NOTE: **Twitter Hashtags**
>
> Hashtags were initiated by Twitter, the social network that now owns Vine. Twitter's official description notes that "the # symbol, called a hashtag, is used to mark keywords or topics in a Tweet. It was created organically by Twitter users as a way to categorize messages."

Adding Hashtags to Your Videos

Vine makes it easy to include hashtags in your video descriptions—if you know how.

Including a Hashtag in the Caption

You add hashtags to the caption that accompanies each video you post to Vine. Hashtags can be included within the normal text description (as words within a sentence) or added to the end of the description, to be viewed in a freestanding manner.

Follow these steps to add hashtags to a caption:

1. Tap the camera button at the top-right of the Home, Explore, or Activity screens to enter recording mode.

2. Tap and hold the screen to begin recording the vine; raise your finger to stop recording.

3. When the preview screen appears, tap the green checkmark to display the Share screen.

4. Use the onscreen keyboard to enter a description of the video into the Add a Caption box, shown in Figure 10.1.

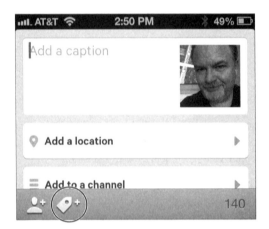

FIGURE 10.1   Entering a caption and hashtags.

5. Enter the hashtag as part of the video's caption. Enter the # character followed by the keyword or keywords for the hashtag.

TIP: **Two Ways to Hash**

You can enter the hash character from the onscreen keyboard, or by tapping the Hash ("tag") icon above the keyboard.

---

6. Complete the posting of the video as normal.

Tips for More Effective Hashtags

It's important to use hashtags properly, and not to overuse them. There are two ways to incorporate hashtags within a caption.

The first approach is to include hashtags within the normal text description, by replacing the normal word with a hashtag, like this:

This is a video about #cutecats.

You can also add hashtags to the end of the normal description, like this:

This is a video about cute cats. #cutecats

Both approaches are equally valid, and equally common.

In addition, you should consider these tips for proper hashtag usage:

- ▶ You can include multiple hashtags in a single caption. However, you shouldn't include too many hashtags; more than two or three verges on hashtag overkill.

- ▶ Make sure your hashtags are relevant to the video you've recorded. If you're just using hashtags to attract searchers, irrelevant to your video's content, you're spamming.

- ▶ Check how a given hashtag is used before you use it. Search for that hashtag, or click it in another video to see what types of videos are similarly tagged—and make sure you're properly using that hashtag.

Searching Vine with Hashtags

One of the chief uses of hashtags is to find other videos with similar content. To that end, you can search Vine for a given hashtag, or just click a hashtag to see similar videos.

Searching Hashtags

Because a hashtag is essentially a searchable keyword, it's easy to search Vine for videos tagged with a particular hashtag. Follow these steps:

1. Tap the Menu button and select Explore to display the Explore page.

2. Enter a keyword into the Search box at the top of the page. You do *not* have to enter the # symbol before the keyword.

3. When the two tabs appear, as shown in Figure 10.2, tap the Tags tab.

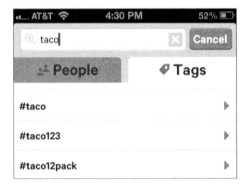

FIGURE 10.2   Searching for hashtags.

4. As you type, Vine displays a list of suggested hashtags. Tap the hashtag you'd like to view.

5. Vine displays a page of videos that contain the desired hashtag. Scroll down the page to view more tagged videos.

Displaying Related Videos

If you're viewing a video that you really like, and that video includes hashtags in its description, you can display similar videos by tapping a hashtag. Follow these steps:

1. Scroll to the caption beneath the video. Check to see whether the caption includes a hashtag—typically displayed in green, as shown in Figure 10.3.

FIGURE 10.3   Tappable hashtags in a video description.

2. Tap the hashtag.

3. Vine displays additional videos tagged with that same hashtag. (The hashtag itself is displayed at the top of the following page.) Scroll down the page to view more.

TIP: **Return to Original**

To return to the original video, tap the back arrow at the top-left corner of the screen.

---

4. To return to the original video, tap the back arrow at the top-left corner of the screen.

Summary

In this lesson, you learned how to add hashtags to your Vine videos, and how to use hashtags to find similar videos.

LESSON 11

Sharing Your Vine

In this lesson, you learn how to revine and to share the Vine videos you create—to Twitter, Facebook, and YouTube.

Sharing New Vines to Social Media

Vine is all about sharing the short videos you create. To that end, Vine is well integrated with the two largest social media today, which makes it easy to share your videos via Twitter and Facebook.

Sharing a New Vine to Twitter

You can share a link to any Vine video via Twitter. When someone clicks the link in your tweet, the video opens and begins to play.

Follow these steps to share a vine via Twitter:

1. Shoot a new video as usual and proceed to the Share screen, shown in Figure 11.1.

2. Check the Twitter option.

3. Select other options on the Share screen as necessary.

4. Tap the Done button.

NOTE: **Shooting a Vine**
Learn more about creating new videos in Lesson 8, "Shooting a Vine."

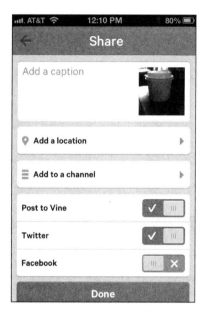

FIGURE 11.1   Sharing a new vine from the Share screen.

Sharing a New Vine to Facebook

You can also share a new vine to your Facebook feed. When someone clicks the video thumbnail in your status update, they play the video.

Follow these steps to share a vine via Facebook:

1. Shoot a new video as usual and proceed to the Share screen.

2. Check the Facebook option.

3. Select other options on the Share screen as necessary.

4. Tap the Done button.

> NOTE: **Connecting to Facebook**
>
> Before you can share vines to Facebook, you have to connect your Facebook and Vine accounts. Learn more in Lesson 4, "Personalizing Vine."

Sharing Existing Vines to Social Media

Vine also lets you share *any* video to Twitter and Facebook, even videos uploaded by other users. This is what makes Vine a particularly social site; when you share videos you like, you help them go viral.

Sharing an Existing Vine to Twitter

Any video you find on Vine can be shared with your Twitter followers. Follow these steps:

1. Navigate to the video you want to share.

2. Tap the More (three dots) button, shown in Figure 11.2.

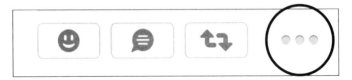

FIGURE 11.2   Tap the More button to display sharing options.

3. When the More panel appears, tap Share This Post.

4. When the Share panel appears, as shown in Figure 11.3, tap the Twitter button.

5. When the Tweet screen appears, as shown in Figure 11.4, accept the existing description or write your own message in the text box.

6. Tap the Done button to share a link to this video in a tweet.

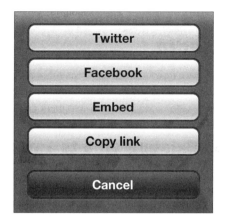

FIGURE 11.3   Sharing a new vine from the Share screen.

FIGURE 11.4   Tweeting a vine.

Sharing an Existing Vine to Facebook

You can also share any existing vine—your own, or other users'—in a Facebook status update. Follow these steps:

1. Navigate to the video you want to share.

2. Tap the More button to display the more panel.

3. Tap the Share This Post button to display the Share panel.

4. Tap the Facebook button.

5. When the Facebook screen appears, as shown in Figure 11.5, accept the existing description or write your own message in the text box.

FIGURE 11.5 Sharing a vine to Facebook.

6. Tap the Done button to share a link to this video to your Facebook feed.

Revining a Vine

Just as Twitter lets you "retweet" an existing tweet, so does Vine let you "revine" any vine on its site. When you revine a vine, you share it with your Vine followers. This way, you can share the vines you like with the people who follow you.

To revine a video to your followers, follow these steps:

1. Navigate to the video you want to share.

2. Tap the Revine button, shown in Figure 11.6.

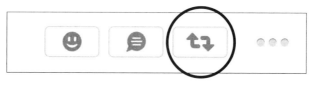

FIGURE 11.6   Revining a vine.

This video now appears on the Home screen of anyone following you on Vine.

Sharing via Email

Vine also lets you use email to send a link to any of its videos to anyone you know. More specifically, you send a link to the vine's Embed Post page—which also includes a live version of the video for online viewing.

Follow these steps:

1. Navigate to the video you want to share.

2. Tap the More button to display the More panel.

3. Tap the Share This Post button.

4. When the Share panel appears, tap the Embed button.

5. When the new message screen appears, as shown in Figure 11.7, enter the recipient's email address into the To: field.

6. Tap the Send button.

The recipient receives an email that includes a link to your vine's Embed Post page. When she clicks the link, she sees information about embedding the vine, as well as the Vine video itself. Playback begins when the recipient clicks the video.

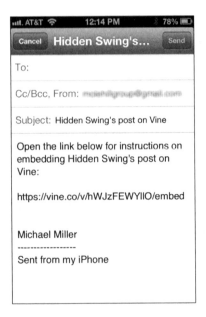

FIGURE 11.7   Sending a link to a vine via email.

TIP: **Display the Viewing Page**

Although you can watch a video from the Embed Post page, a better viewing experience can be had from the video's dedicated viewing page. To display this page, take the Embed Post page's URL and remove the **/embed** from the end. This gives you the URL for the video-viewing page.

Sharing to YouTube

Vine automatically uploads your videos to its own service. As you just learned, Vine also lets you link to your uploaded videos from Twitter and Facebook. But you can also upload your vines to YouTube, the web's largest video-sharing service.

Every Vine video you shoot is saved as a QuickTime .mov file in your phone' or tablet's camera roll. You can upload these small video files to YouTube by following these steps:

1. Open your device's camera roll.

2. Tap to open the video you want to upload.

3. Tap the video to display the options bar, then tap the Share icon, shown in Figure 11.8.

FIGURE 11.8   Tap the Share icon in your phone's camera roll.

4. Tap the YouTube icon, shown in Figure 11.9.

FIGURE 11.9   Tap the YouTube icon to share the video to YouTube.

5. When the Publish Video screen appears, as shown in Figure 11.10, enter a title for the video into the Title field.

6. Enter a short description of the video into the Description field.

7. Enter one or more keywords that describe the video's content into the Tags field.

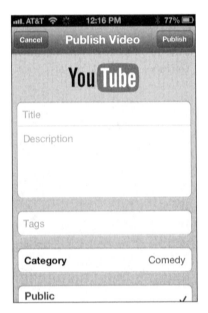

FIGURE 11.10   Adding information to the video description.

8. Tap the Category field and select a category for the video.

9. Tap the Publish button to upload the video to your YouTube account.

TIP: **Uploading to Other Sites**

Because Vine stores each video you create on your mobile device, you can share these files to any video-sharing service. You first have to download or import the individual file from your phone or tablet to your computer, using either Windows or the Mac OS. After the video file is safely stored on your computer's hard drive, you can then upload that file to your video-sharing service of choice, using that site's recommended procedure.

Summary

In this lesson, you learned how to share Vine videos with others via Twitter, Facebook, YouTube, and email. You also learned how to revine your favorite videos to your Vine followers.

LESSON 12

Planning Your Vine

In this lesson, you discover how to plan for more effective videos.

Why Planning is Important

Some terrific Vine videos emerge on the spur of the moment. Most of the better videos, however, are planned in advance. In fact, pre-vine planning is the key to creating more effective (and better viewed and reviewed) videos.

Given Vine's six-second limit, it's important to make the best use of those six seconds; you literally don't have a second to waste. That means planning everything that gets recorded, from the first word or movement to the last. With so little time to shoot everything you want, you can't leave anything to chance.

Planning is especially important if you want to incorporate multiple shots in your videos. Remember, you can't edit your Vine videos; there's no way to stitch together multiple takes or shots from a pool of different video files. The only way to do it is to shoot one shot after another, pausing only to change camera angle or move the subject around.

Different types of videos require more planning than others. If you're just shooting a single-shot selfie, maybe you don't need a whole lot of prep work. But if you're shooting a complex multi-shot how-to video (in six seconds, nonetheless), you need to plan exactly what's included in each shot. Same thing if you're doing a stop-action video; every frame needs to be planned in advance. In short, the more you have happening in your video, the more planning you need.

No matter what type of video you're shooting, however, you always have to deal with the time issue. If you don't plan carefully, you'll run out of time; six seconds is not long at all. Plan your shots, even if it's just a single shot, carefully, and down to the split second. After all, you don't want your video to cut off in the middle of a sentence.

> CAUTION: **No Editing**
>
> Planning is also important because you can't go back and edit your Vine video after you start recording. If you shoot something wrong in the middle, your only option is to go back and reshoot from the beginning.

Before You Start...

Before you start planning, you need to know why you're shooting this video, and for whom you're shooting it. It's a matter of determining what you're trying to do before you do it.

Setting a Goal

Why are you recording this video? That's the first question you should ask before you even launch the Vine app. What do you hope to accomplish—what's the desired end result?

Maybe you want to inform viewers about a given issue. Maybe you want to show them how to do something. Maybe you just want to entertain them, have a little fun. All of these are valid goals.

Your goal can be as broad as "make people laugh" or as focused as "demonstrate how to make an origami bird." The point is to know what you want to achieve with your vine, which then helps to focus your activity to meet that goal.

TIP: **One Goal**
You should focus on a single goal for your video. If you try to make one video do multiple things (especially a short six-second video), you're unlikely to accomplish any of them. Set one thing you want to do with the video, and then do it.

Determining Your Target Audience

In conjunction with determining why you're shooting this video, ask yourself *who* you're shooting it for. What entertains a college-aged gamer is likely to completely turn off a thirty-something housewife. One size video definitely does not fit all potential viewers.

When you identify a target audience for your video, you'll know a little bit more about how you video should look, and what kind of content it should contain. Make the video appeal to the target audience, in terms of look and feel. A younger audience appreciates a rougher, more immediate approach; older viewers might want something slicker and more professional looking. Know who your target viewer is, and you'll know what kind of video to deliver.

That also goes for your video's content. If your target audience consists of beginning cooks, you know to provide basic kitchen information. If, on the other hand, your audience is full of experienced chefs, you should offer more in-depth culinary content. Find out what your audience knows, what they don't know, and what they need or want to know, and then give it to them.

NOTE: **Vines for Business**
Many companies are embracing Vine as a way to promote their products and connect to their customers. For example, Lowe's has a series of how-to vines for its DIY customers; General Electric uses stop-motion animation to present its various products and services; and Target offers a number of entertaining vines to push its brand and stores. Search for your favorite company on Vine to see how they're using six-second videos to reach their customer base.

Telling a Story

When it comes to planning your video, think in terms of telling a story. Storytelling is an effective way to get your point across, especially in six short seconds.

Everyone can relate to a story. Since the beginning of time, information has been passed from person to person via stories. The narrative structure helps to draw in the audience, involve them in the action, and convey important information.

Stories can be verbal, written, or visual. They can also be told via video—which is where Vine comes in. With Vine, you have six seconds to tell a story that engages your target audience, conveys the desired information, and achieves your stated goal.

> NOTE: **Non Stories**
> Not all Vine videos tell a story. Sometimes you just want to capture the moment or establish a mood, neither one of which requires a plot or protagonist. That's okay; vines can be used in many different ways.

The Parts of a Story

The story you tell should have the following components:

▶ **Characters.** These are the people in your video. Characters perform the action in your video; they do what needs to be done. You can have a single character or multiple characters; probably no more than two, however, given Vine's six-second limitation. If you use multiple characters, one should play the role of the main character, or protagonist, to whom things happen.

▶ **Setting.** This is where your video takes place, the location of the action. Taking Vine's six-second rule into account, your story probably has a single location—although you can employ multiple locations if you want.

▶ **Plot.** This is the actual story within your video. A plot should have a clear beginning, middle, and end—even in a six-second video. You get something started, you do it, then you finish.

▶ **Conflict.** All good stories present some sort of conflict that must be solved. In a how-to video, the conflict is the task that must be accomplished. In an informational video, it's the reason that information is needed.

▶ **Resolution.** When you solve your conflict, you have your resolution. It's the solution to your problem, how things get worked out—and, typically, the very end of your vine.

How do these elements translate to a six-second Vine video? Easier than you might suspect.

Let's say you're shooting a video showing how to fry an egg. The person doing the frying (even if you only see her hands) is the lead character. The setting is your kitchen stovetop. The plot is how to cook an egg. The conflict is the need to cook the egg. The resolution is the successful cooking of said egg.

How about a selfie—a video of you talking directly to the camera? You, obviously, are the lead character. The setting is wherever you happen to be sitting. The plot is the message you want to convey. The conflict is why you need to get the message out. The resolution is your final statement.

You need all these elements, no matter how brief or self-evident, to create a successful video.

How to Tell Your Story

Vine gives you a whopping six seconds to tell your story, so you need to be very concise in your storytelling. You don't have time for a leisurely setup; get started quickly and work as efficiently as possible.

That said, there are many ways to tell a story. You can literally *tell* the story, with the subject (you or someone else) talking on camera. You can *show* the story, without words, using various items in various shots. You can even act out the story, using multiple shots and (perhaps) multiple subjects.

Pick the approach that best fits what you hope to accomplish, and that is best suited for your target audience. There's no one right way to do it; tackle the topic in the way you deem best.

Creating Scripts and Storyboards

How exactly do you plan out a video? You can do it in either words or pictures.

Writing a Script

A script is a text-based breakdown of all the shots, action, and dialogue for your video. Each shot should indicate what's being shot, what happens in the shot, and what the speaker or speakers say.

A typical script might look something like this:

SHOT ONE

FRYING PAN, FROM ABOVE

ACTION: TWO HANDS PLACING PAT OF BUTTER INTO PAN

NARRATOR: Grease a hot frying pan with butter or olive oil.

SHOT TWO

FRYING PAN, FROM ABOVE

ACTION: TWO HANDS CRACKING EGG INTO FRYING PAN

NARRATOR: Gently crack one egg into the pan.

SHOT THREE

FRYING PAN, FROM ABOVE

ACTION: SPATULA MOVING EGG AROUND PAN

NARRATOR: Cook for about a minute, seasoning with salt and pepper.

SHOT FOUR

EMPTY PLATE, FROM ABOVE

ACTION: SPATULA SLIDING EGG FROM PAN ONTO PLATE

NARRATOR: Slide the cooked egg onto a plate and enjoy!

Constructing a Storyboard

Given the visual nature of Vine videos, you might want to create a storyboard in addition to or instead of a written script. A *storyboard* is a series of pictures that sketch out what is seen in each shot. Write the narration for that shot beneath each thumbnail.

Figure 12.1 shows a typical storyboard. The thumbnails do not have to be overly detailed, nor particularly artistic. They only need to convey what you want to show in each shot; rough sketches are perfectly acceptable.

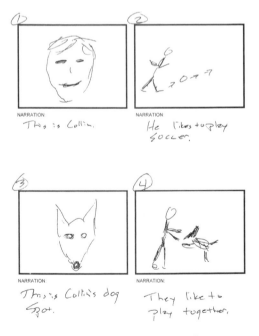

FIGURE 12.1   Create a storyboard to outline your shots.

Think of a storyboard as a kind of visual outline. Line up your camera until you see what you drew for each thumbnail, then record. It's a great roadmap to help create the video you want.

Summary

In this lesson, you learned how to plan your video, tell a story, and create scripts and storyboards.

LESSON 13

Shooting People

In this lesson, you learn how to shoot Vine videos with people in them—including yourself.

Shooting Other People

Many vines are recordings of people—people talking, people moving, people doing some thing or another. Shooting an effective "people" video isn't quite as simple as aiming at a person and tapping the screen to record; there are some helpful techniques you can employ to create better vines.

Shooting a Talking Head

It sounds easy. Hold your device's camera in front of a person, tap the screen, and have her start talking. Well, shooting a single person (what we call a *talking head* video) comes with its own unique set of challenges. If you're not careful, you'll record six seconds of a shaky dark blob blathering unintelligibly about who knows what.

Here's what you need to do to shoot an effective talking head video, one that looks and sounds as good as possible.

▶ **Fill the screen.** Hold your device's camera relatively close to the person you're filming, just a few feet away. You don't want a full body shot; instead, you want the person's head and shoulders to fill the screen. Get much closer and the big head gets a little scary. Get too much further away and you can't see the guy's lips move. (Figure 13.1, later in this lesson, shows the right way to do this.)

▶ **Position the subject off-center.** For a more interesting visual, don't position the subject dead center in the screen. Move the person slightly to the right or left, using the rule of thirds to create a more sophisticated composition.

▶ **Vary the shots.** If your video includes more than one shot, you may want to vary the positioning and angle of the subject between shots, much the way newscasts shoot the anchor from the front and from a slightly side angle. It breaks up the visual monotony.

▶ **Light from the front or side.** You want to be able to see the person's face. That means positioning her so that the available light shines face on. For a more interesting effect, position the light slightly to the side; this creates dramatic shadows on the person's face. Ideally, you want the camera slightly in front of whatever light source you're using.

TIP: **Use External Lighting**

If the available light isn't bright enough, the video will be dark and grainy. You might want to supplement the existing light with some sort of external lighting, either from a professional lighting kit, or just another light in the room. Learn more about external lighting in Lesson 17, "Using Accessories for Better Vines."

CAUTION: **Avoid Backlighting**

Camera phones don't handle multiple lighting sources all that well. To that end, avoid *backlighting*, or any light behind the subject. Your camera is likely to get confused and record the subject in relative darkness.

▶ **Use a simple background.** You want viewers to focus on your subject, not what's behind him. To that end, avoid busy or distracting backgrounds—and never, ever shoot in front of an open window. Instead, use a plain neutral-colored background, so that the subject "pops" in front of it.

▶ **Keep the camera stable.** When shooting a talking head video, you want the image to be rock solid. Although you can try to steady the camera by holding your elbows into the sides of your body, you might be better off laying the side of the camera on a hard surface or by using a tripod. (Learn more about tripods in Lesson 17.)

Shooting a Conversation

Follow these tips and shooting one person is relatively easy. But what do you do when you have two people in the video?

There are several different ways to approach two-person videos. Here are your options:

▶ **Shoot both people in the same shot, looking at each other.** When done right (and if you can get both heads in the shot), this looks as if you're shooting an actual conversation. It's the pre-ferred approach when the two people are having a real dialog.

> TIP: **Cheat the Angle**
> Instead of having each person look exactly at each other, they can "cheat" the shot a little to look slightly towards the camera, instead. This helps to personalize the shot, as well as show more of each person's face rather than stark side shots.

▶ **Shoot both people in the same shot, looking at the camera.** This is the way to go if each person is presenting separate points, rather than engaging in a true dialog. Each person talks directly to the camera in turn.

▶ **Record each person separately, one after another.** This might be the most effective way to get up close and personal with each participant in the conversation. It's easy enough to do with the Vine app; just tap to record the first person talking, pause, then tap to record the second person talking. Repeat as often as necessary to capture the complete conversation. You can have

each person talking directly to the camera, or have them facing
left and right, as if they're talking to each other.

Remember to follow the same general guidelines when shooting two people as when shooting one. Watch your framing, lighting, and background
to shoot each of the two people as appealingly as possible.

CAUTION: **Tighten It Up**

Try to avoid too much empty space at the beginning and end of each
person's part of the conversation. You want the video to be as tight
as possible, without unnecessary pauses and transitions.

Shooting a Group of People

Shooting a group of people is a little more difficult when using a camera
phone. That's because you need to frame more people in a relatively small
space. Get too far away and you won't see individual faces. Get too close
and you'll crop people out of the shot.

This means you might need to make some difficult choices. Do you need
to include the entire group in the frame? Should you attempt a more formal composition, the better to squeeze more people into a smaller space?
Should you isolate the shot on one or two key people, following them
while the rest of the group is relegated to wallpaper status?

The use of multiple shots might be the best approach here. Shoot an initial
establishing shot of the entire group, then focus your next shots on key
individuals. End the video with another shot of the entire group. With this
approach, the viewer sees that there's a large group of people present, but
then is presented directly with the key players close up.

Shooting an Action Shot

Shooting people becomes even more challenging when those people are
moving. Maybe you're shooting a football game, maybe you're shooting
some people walking, maybe you're shooting friends at a pool. In any of
these situations, you need to keep the main subject(s) close to center
frame, while moving the camera to capture the action.

If you can, shoot the action moving from left to right. That's how we read and how we expect things to move. So shoot your subjects walking from left to right, or kicking the ball from the left side of the frame to the right, or even diving into the pool from left to right.

TIP: Zooming

Even though the Vine Android app includes a zoom feature, it's difficult to use while shooting and isn't a real optical zoom; it's a digital zoom that can result in a pixelated picture. If you want to zoom in while shooting, the better approach is to simply walk closer to what you're shooting.

Shooting a Selfie

One of the most popular types of videos on Vine is the *selfie*—a video of yourself. Think of a selfie as your own personal talking head, your chance to say a few words directly to the camera.

Most selfies are shot using the phone's front-facing camera. This requires you to tap the Switch Camera button from the shooting screen, as shown in Figure 13.1 (and described in Lesson 8, "Shooting a Vine"). Hold the camera at arm's length or so, smile, and then tap the screen to start recording.

The problem with shooting a selfie by yourself is that it's difficult to hold the camera steady. You'll get better results if you can lay the camera on a stable surface, or even use a tripod.

Even if you use a tripod, you still have to reach out to tap the screen to record. If you find this a trifle tricky, you might need to enlist a friend to help you shoot your selfies. (I know, having someone else shoot you seemingly contradicts the notion of a selfie, but there you go.) When someone else is holding and operating the camera, you're relieved of those responsibilities and can focus on your narration or monologue. You also don't have to worry about holding the camera steady or keeping your arm out of the shot.

FIGURE 13.1 Tap the Switch Camera button to shoot a selfie with your phone's front-facing camera.

Of course, when you're shooting yourself you still need to keep in mind all the tips for shooting other people. Hold the camera close enough so that your face fills the frame, avoid backlighting, don't stand in front of anything distracting, and the like.

CAUTION: **Stay Still**

Although you *can* walk around while you're shooting a selfie (assuming you're coordinated enough to walk and talk at the same time), that might not be a good idea. The moving background behind you could prove too distracting for your viewers.

Summary

In this lesson, you learned how to capture yourself and other people in Vine videos.

LESSON 14

Shooting a How-To

In this lesson, you learn how to use Vine to create how-to videos, in six seconds or less.

How to Plan a How-To Video— Step-by-Step

Six seconds isn't a lot of time to show someone how to do something, but it can be done. In fact, how-to videos are some of the most popular videos on Vine.

Before you attempt to shoot a how-to video, however, you need to do a little planning. It's a real challenge to cram a lot of steps into six little seconds.

Understanding How-To Videos

A how-to video is just what the name implies, a video that shows you how to do something. How-to videos (and books, for that matter) lay out what you need to do to accomplish a specific task, in a step-by-step series of instructions. That is, you start with step one, move to step two, and so forth, until the task is completed.

You can use how-to videos to show how to do just about anything— although Vine's six-second limitation might keep you from describing overly complex tasks. Search Vine for the hashtag **#howto** and you find videos that show how to play the piano, put on makeup, assemble a DIY lamp, get a tan, cook hamburgers, and on and on. Just about any topic is rife for a how-to video; if you know how to do something, you can use Vine to show other people how to do it, too.

Laying Out the Steps

Any task can be explained via step-by-step instructions. It's a matter of breaking the task into discrete steps. Do this first, then do that, then do the next thing. It's a matter of thinking in terms of one-two-three.

Consider the task of grilling a hamburger. Imagine yourself talking a friend through the process:

"Pre-heat your grill to a high heat, then put the patties directly on the grill. Flip them over after about three minutes. Give 'em another three minutes on the other side, then they're done."

Now convert these spoken words into a series of numbered steps. You'll get something like this:

1. Pre-heat your grill to a high heat.

2. Place the patties directly on the grill.

3. After three minutes on the first side, flip the burgers.

4. After three minutes on the second side, the burgers are done.

TIP: Preparation

Note that these instructions do not include the preparatory steps of buying the ground beef and forming the patties. You may or may not need to include such preparatory instructions; it all depends on your audience. The less your audience knows, the more you have to tell them. Likewise, if you're dealing with a more experienced audience, you might be able to skip or assume a step or two.

Just about any task can be broken down into its component parts like this. Just think about each individual thing you need to do, and make that a discrete step in your instructions.

Adapting Instructions for a Six-Second Vine

Although just about any task can be described in step-by-step instructions, not every task is suited to the Vine app. You need a task that's visual and that can be explained in six seconds or less. If a task is too long or too complex, you won't be able to fully show how to do it.

> TIP: **YouTube**
> Longer or more complex tasks are better suited to the longer how-to videos found on YouTube and similar video-sharing sites.

Converting Steps to Shots

If the task is short enough, it's a simple task to represent each written step as a separate shot in a Vine video. Just shoot each step as a single shot, being as economical as possible with your time.

Let's take our burger-grilling example and present it in a shot-by-shot fashion, as such:

SHOT ONE

FRONT OF GRILL

ACTION: HAND TURNING KNOB TO "HIGH"

NARRATOR: Pre-heat your grill to high.

SHOT TWO

OPEN GRILL

ACTION: HAND PLACING PATTY ON GRILL

NARRATOR: Place your patties directly on the grill.

SHOT THREE

BURGERS ON GRILL

ACTION: SPATULA FLIPPING BURGER

NARRATOR: Cook for three minutes on each side.

SHOT FOUR

BURGERS ON GRILL

ACTION: SPATULA REMOVING BURGER FROM GRILL

NARRATOR: After three minutes on the second side, your burgers are done.

And that is your shooting script. Four simple shots that easily fit in a six-second video.

NOTE: **Timing**

Your step-by-step instructions do not have to be presented in real time. Although it might take six minutes to actually cook a burger, you can show the individual steps in six seconds by leaving out those long segments where you're not actually doing anything.

Four steps is about right for a six-second vine. If you can show how to do something in fewer steps (without leaving out anything important), great. But you'll find it difficult to fit more than a half-dozen steps into the six-second timeframe. You need to give each step at least a second to sink in for the viewer.

That means that you might not have time for all your steps. You might need to condense two or more steps into a single step to fit within Vine's time constraints. Perhaps you can imply missing instructions, or even say them in your narration while you show another step onscreen. You'll need to be creative in your use of time to fit everything in.

That also means that you probably won't have time for introductions and summations, nor for title cards or credits. As far as Vine is concerned, you have to jump into a how-to video with your feet running. Your first shot should be the first step and then you tumble through the rest from there.

> TIP: **Title in the Description**
> Use your vine's caption to tell viewers what the video is about. If your video is a how-to for grilling burgers, say something like **#Grilling #burgers #howto**. (Note the use of hashtags in the description.)

Show, Don't Tell

Words can sometimes slow you down. That is, you can often show how to do something faster than you can tell someone how to do it.

To that end, many how-to vines are visual only, with no accompanying narration. If you're demonstrating how to paint your nails, for example, you don't need a running description to show what needs to be done; just shoot yourself painting your nails and that'll do.

> CAUTION: **Time for Words**
> Presenting a how-to in pictures only, without words, works only if the task itself is not time sensitive, or if you can show the steps in real time. Our burger cooking how-to, for example, needs a narration to tell people how long to cook per side.

Let's look at a vine that shows how to plant a tulip bulb. You can do it without words, as in the following shooting script:

SHOT ONE

EMPTY SPOT IN GARDEN

ACTION: TROWEL DIGGING HOLE, TWICE THE SIZE OF BULB

SHOT TWO

NEW HOLE IN GARDEN

ACTION: HAND PLACING TULIP BULB INTO HOLE, TIP POINT-
ING UPWARDS

SHOT THREE

BULB IN HOLE

ACTION: HANDS PLACING SOIL ON TOP OF BULB

That's a three-step video, no verbal instructions necessary. The three shots
tell the entire story; adding narration would only slow things down.

Plan It Out

Planning is essential to an effective how-to video. You need to know the
steps involved, and how you plan to shoot each step.

This argues in favor of creating a storyboard for your video. The thumbnails in the storyboard should detail each of the three or four steps you
need to shoot.

Shoot the Video

After you've created your storyboard, it's time to shoot the video.
Shooting a how-to video is typically a two-person job. One person holds
the camera phone or tablet and stops and starts recording; the second person is the on-air talent, performing the necessary tasks for the camera.

As with all Vine videos, your how-to will benefit from a steady camera,
which means employing a tripod. Make sure the lighting is good (you
want to be able to see whatever it is you're demonstrating) and that the
camera position clearly shows the task being performed.

> NOTE: **Accessories**
> Learn more about external lights and tripods in Lesson 17, "Using
> Accessories for Better Vines."

If you don't get it right the first go-round, delete the video and shoot it again. It's important that you get all the steps right; remember, other people will be following—and depending upon—your instructions.

Summary

In this lesson, you learned how to plan and shoot how-to videos.

Creating a Stop Motion Video

In this lesson, you learn how to create stop motion videos in Vine.

Understanding Stop Motion Animation

Some of the most interesting Vine videos use multiple single-frame shots to create a stop motion effect. This is the type of animation that you've seen in numerous cartoons and movies, from the original *King Kong* and various fantasy films animated by the legendary Ray Harryhausen, to more modern efforts such as the *Rudolph the Red-Nosed Reindeer* holiday special, the Wallace and Gromit cartoons from Aardman Animations, and the *Robot Chicken* TV show.

A stop motion video is composed of multiple shots, each a frame or so in length. The subjects in the video, typically inanimate objects made of clay or paper, are moved ever so slightly from shot to shot. The result is a brief animation, with the objects moving in a relatively smooth fashion from beginning to end.

There are lots of stop motion videos on Vine; just search for the **#stopmotion** hashtag to see a sampling. You can also follow some of the more imaginative posters who employ the stop motion technique, such as Khoa Phan, Ian Padgham, Mark Weaver, and Meagan Cignoli.

Khoa Phan, as an example, creates his videos using colorful shapes cut out of construction paper. His stop motion animation gives the illusion that the shapes and characters are moving across a table, as shown in

Figure 15.1, often to reveal a final message. His fun stop motion videos have attracted more than 50,000 followers to date.

FIGURE 15.1 A stop motion video from Khoa Phan, created from construction paper cut-outs.

Ian Padgham's stop motion videos utilize a small wooden artist's model, like the one shown in Figure 15.2. Padgham animates the model to perform various tasks in his videos, making the wooden figure come to life with surprising human-like motions.

Mark Weaver's vines are all about Legos, as you can see in Figure 15.3. He uses stop motion to "build" a Lego structure in each video, seemingly one brick at a time. The result is kind of trippy, with colorful patterns appearing and disappearing over the course of each six-second vine.

FIGURE 15.2 A stop motion video from Ian Padgham, using a wooden artist's model.

FIGURE 15.3 One of Mark Weaver's Lego stop motion vines.

Meagan Cignoli doesn't limit herself to any single style of stop motion in her vines. Some feature inanimate objects, and others feature real people moving slightly from shot to shot, as shown in Figure 15.4. There's a wealth of creativity there.

FIGURE 15.4   A real person in one of Meagan Cignoli's stop motion vines.

NOTE: **Brands and Products**

Many companies are using stop motion vines to promote their brands and products. Examples include Etsy, Lowe's, Red Vines (candy), and Target.

Preparing a Stop Motion Vine

All you need to create a stop motion vine is your camera phone or tablet, something to keep it steady throughout the shooting, and something small you can move and shoot. A little imagination also helps—as does a lot of planning.

You can't really shoot an off-the-cuff stop motion video. You need to know what's moving where and when, one step at a time. You have to plan out each individual frame, moving the object(s) slowly and steadily over the course of the video.

For most Vinesters, that means storyboarding your video one frame at a time. You can do this via a series of brief sketches that detail what moves (and where) in each shot. When it comes time to shoot the video, you just follow the sketches you've made to slightly move each object from frame to frame.

Shooting in Stop Motion

The key to shooting a stop motion vine is patience. You might shoot several dozen individual shots, with the object(s) you're shooting moving a fraction of an inch from shot to shot. That requires a lot of patience on your part.

You also need to keep your camera phone or tablet perfectly still throughout the video. You can't do this if you're holding the device; you'll never be able to keep it in exactly the same space from shot to shot.

This argues for using some sort of device to lock your camera phone or tablet in one place. The best approach is to use a tripod, but you can also jerry rig a stationary camera with duct tape if need be. You might also want to consider the use of a remote shutter trigger device, which results in less camera shake than tapping the screen.

> NOTE: **Accessories**
> Learn more about the accessories you need to keep your camera steady in Lesson 17, "Using Accessories for Better Vines."

It's also important to keep the lighting constant from shot to shot. That probably means using some sort of artificial lighting, as sunlight will change over time as the sun moves across the sky (or as clouds move in front of the sun). Position your lighting where you want it and then don't move it—and don't walk in front of it during a shot.

> TIP: **Use the Ghost Function**
> Vine's Ghost function is designed specifically to help users shoot stop motion videos. Tap the Ghost button while shooting to see a ghost image of your previous shot. Use this ghost image to better align the next slightly different shot in a stop motion video.

When it comes to time shoot the video, you need to master the art of single-tapping the screen of the Vine app. Each tap records a very short piece of video, which is exactly what you need to capture a stop motion frame. Don't tap and hold, just tap and release. The shorter you tap the screen, the smoother the animation will be.

The process, then, is as follows:

1. Set up the objects in your first shot.

2. Tap the screen to record a fraction of a second of video.

3. Move the objects a very small amount.

4. Tap the screen to record another fraction of a second of video.

5. Repeat steps 3 and 4 until you've completed the video.

In other words, it's move-tap-move-tap-move-tap until you're done. When you preview the video, you'll see the objects moving across the screen, as designed. The shorter each tap—and the less movement there is from shot to shot—the smoother the animation effect will be.

> CAUTION: **It's a Long Process**
> It takes a very long time to record six seconds of stop motion animation. Unlike a normal vine, where you record six seconds in near real time, it might take you an hour or more to shoot six seconds of stop motion.

As practice, try animating a ball moving across the screen from left to right. Position the ball at the far left side of the frame, then tap the screen. Move the ball a fraction of an inch to the right, then tap the screen again. Move the ball another fraction of an inch, then tap the screen again. Keep repeating until either the ball has moved to the right side of the frame or you've expended your six seconds of recording. The result should look as if the ball is rolling from left to right.

For more practice, try animating two Hot Wheels cars. Position one at the top-left corner of the frame and the other at the top-right corner of the frame. Your video will have the cars moving toward the center of the frame, where they will crash together and then turn over. Move each car down and to the center a fraction of an inch, tap the screen, and repeat until they meet in the middle. Now you can slowly turn the cars over, shot by shot, until they're lying upside down. The result, when you play it back, should look like a cool little car crash.

Summary

In this lesson, you learned how to create stop motion Vine videos.

LESSON 16

Creating the Perfect Loop

In this lesson, you learn how to create Vine videos that loop perfectly back to the start.

What's a Loop?

Vines are looping videos—that is, they play continuously from start to finish and back to start again. Because of this constantly repeating nature, watching a vine can be a bit of a jarring experience if the end doesn't match back up to the beginning.

It's important, then, to recognize the looping nature of Vine videos, and to plan your videos around that repetition. The best vines are infinite loops, where you can't tell where the video begins and where it ends. (The worst, by implication, are those that have an abrupt ending that doesn't relate at all to the beginning.)

To accomplish a perfect loop, you need the last frame of your video to lead seamlessly back to the first frame. That is, the beginning of your first shot and the end of your last shot should be near identical. The test is if viewers, coming in during the middle, can't tell where the beginning and endpoints are.

Some of the best loops come from the same people who make some of the best stop motion vines, such as Meagan Cignoli, Ian Padgham, and Khoa Phan. You should also check out the looping work from users Jethro Ames, Yves Das, and Charlie Love.

NOTE: **#loop**

To see more interesting looping videos, search for the hashtags **#loop** and **#perfectloop**.

Jethro Ames' looping videos feature everyday items moving back and forth and changing into other shapes, as shown in Figure 16.1. The stop motion animation is perfectly synchronized so that the last position of the subject leads directly back to the first position in the video.

Jethro Ames   may 7
#howto play with your food.
Elevator edition. #favthings
#Vine

FIGURE 16.1   Jethro Ames' looping vine shows viewers how to play with their food.

Figure 16.2 shows a looping stop motion video from creator Yves Das. Most of Das' works feature a toy motorcycle (with tiny riders) zooming back and forth across an outsized landscape, such as the tube of toothpaste in this example. The motorcycle just keeps riding, over and over, in an infinite loop.

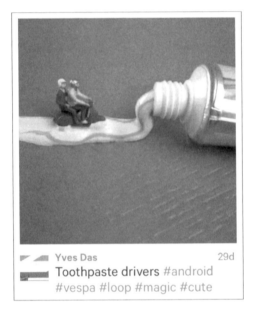

FIGURE 16.2   Yves Das' looping toy motorcycle and riders.

Charlie Love has produced a number of interesting looping videos. I'm particularly fond of the one shown in Figure 16.3 (hashtagged **#vinecation**) where the subject holds up a photograph himself standing in front of the San Francisco City Hall while he's standing in front of the real City Hall. The camera zooms into the photograph, which then loops back to the real thing. It's a trippy effect that's oddly mesmerizing.

Planning a Loop

When planning to shoot a looping video, the key element is matching up the first and last frames—that is, the beginning of your first shot and the end of your last shot. These two frames should either be identical or the last frame should lead naturally back to the first one.

Charlie Love   mar 7
#vinecation #loop
SAN FRANCISCO CITY HALL

FIGURE 16.3   A trippy looping video of the San Francisco City Hall, by vinester Charlie Love.

This isn't as simple as it sounds, but is made easier if you storyboard your video. In addition to making sure that the action flows smoothly from shot to shot, you can also ensure that the final shot—the last screen in your storyboard—is either identical to the first shot or leads naturally back to that shot.

> NOTE: **Storyboards**
> Learn more about storyboards in Lesson 12, "Planning Your Vine."

Let's say you're shooting a ping pong ball bouncing back and forth across the screen, either in real time or in stop motion animation. If your first shot shows the ball bouncing in from the left side of the screen, the final shot should show the ball bouncing from the right to that same spot on the left. The effect, when looped, is of the ball bouncing off the left side of the screen.

Another example: Shoot a friend walking around the perimeter of your back yard. (Assuming your yard is small enough to be walked in six seconds or less, of course.) Position your camera in the middle of the yard and start recording him at a fixed spot. Rotate the camera 360 degrees as he walks around the yard, then stop the recording when he reaches the exact same spot where he started. The last shot of him at this spot should match up with the first shot of him there, with the resulting loop showing him walking over and over and over around your yard.

Still another approach to try: Shoot your hand reaching into a bag of potato chips. Then shoot yourself eating that chip. Then show your hand reaching back into the bag. When looped, you end up eating an infinite bag of chips.

Again, the key is making sure your action flows naturally from the last shot back to the first. The only real way to ensure that this happens is to plan it.

Shooting a Loop

Now we come to the shooting of your loop. Making the perfect loop is really no different than shooting any vine; it just requires a bit more attention to what you put in your first and last shots.

Match Up the First and Last Shots

It goes without saying that to create a smooth loop, the last frame of your final shot has to match up with the first frame of your initial shot. If the shots don't match up, your video will jump when it loops.

This means that whatever is in your first shot has to also be in your final shot. Your main subject, of course, has to line up in both shots, but also any other items in the shot, including the background.

This becomes especially challenging if you're shooting outdoors on a windy day. One tree blowing a little different in the two shots will ruin your looping effect. For that matter, so will "extras" in any crowd shots you might take.

For ease of looping, then, keep the items in your shots as simple as possible. Don't shoot outdoors (or anywhere, for that matter) where the background might move on you. Don't shoot crowds of people. Shoot a minimum of people or items in your first and last shots; the more you have to deal with, the harder it is to line everything up.

> NOTE: **Light**
>
> If you're shooting a multiple shot or stop motion video, make sure that the lighting remains the same for the first and last shots. If the light changes from sunny to cloudy at the looping spot, the entire looping effect will be ruined.

Keep the Camera Steady

It's not just your subjects in the shot that have to match up properly between your first and last shots. You also need to keep your camera in the exact same position for both shots. If the camera is moved, the subject(s) in the shots will be in different positions on playback. That makes for a jarring—and non-loopworthy—video.

The easiest way to repeat the camera angle is to keep the camera completely motionless throughout the entire video. This argues in favor of mounting the camera on a tripod and just leaving it there. This way all your shots—including the first and last—will be perfectly matched.

> NOTE: **Lighting, Tripods, and Audio**
>
> Learn more about lighting, tripods, and audio in Lesson 17, "Using Accessories for Better Vines."

If, on the other hand, you want or need to move the camera throughout the course of the video, you have to take extra care to return the camera to its starting position for the final shot. This is challenging. You need to have a good memory of what you saw on the camera's viewscreen in that initial shot; it helps if you've storyboarded the camera angle so you can duplicate the initial position.

Don't Forget the Audio...

When planning and shooting a looping video, it's understandable to focus on the video, and trying to match up what's onscreen. It's not just the picture that loops, however; you also have to match up the audio from the last frame to the first in a way that sounds natural.

The easiest way to deal with looping audio is to not deal with it—that is, to shoot a silent video. If there's no audio on the soundtrack, you don't have to worry about it matching up.

If you want audio in your video, there are two ways to deal with looping.

First, you can plan for silence at the looping spot. Make sure there's no talking or noise when you tap to record the first shot, and also make sure you're shooting silence at the end of the last shot. Even through there might be talking in the middle of the video, the silence at the beginning and end will ensure there's no jarring audio mismatch when the vine repeats.

Second, you can plan for a clever audio loop, so that the last words or sounds at the end of the video lead back to the words or sounds recorded on the first shot. For example, you could say the word "loop" as you start recording, then make sure your last words in the video are "I am recording a." When looped together, you get "I am recording a loop," and no one will know where things start and end, audio-wise.

This is more difficult when you have other sounds in your video, especially music. With music, the key is making sure the beat lines up during the repeat; ideally, you want to keep the same bar or measure structure, as well. You don't want the music to skip a beat or even half a beat when the video loops. Shoot the video so that the music sounds as if it continuously repeating, as well.

Summary

In this lesson, you learned how to create a smoothly looping Vine video.

LESSON 17

Using Accessories for Better Vines

In this lesson, you learn how to enhance your Vine videos by using various accessories for your camera phone and tablet.

Enhancing the Picture

Depending on what kind of smartphone or tablet you have, the built-in video camera might take a pretty good picture, or it might not. In any case, you can make your videos look better by adding one or more accessories designed to enhance the quality of your video picture.

Keeping It Steady with a Tripod

One of the main problems with camera phone videos is that they're shaky. It's difficult to hold a small phone steady in your hand, and if the camera shakes, you end up with a jumpy video.

The solution is to keep your smartphone perfectly still. Now, you can do this manually, by sitting the camera on a hard surface, or even using duct tape to tie it down so it doesn't move. But the better solution is to mount your phone on some sort of tripod.

Unfortunately, you can't use a traditional camera tripod because your smartphone doesn't include a screw-on mount on the bottom. Fortunately, several companies have come up with other ways to mount a phone to a tripod, which makes it easy to create rock-steady Vine videos.

The most popular tripods for smartphone use are the Gorillapod line from Joby (www.joby.com/smartphones/). Joby makes several different models, with the most suitable for Vine use being the GripTight GorillaPod Video, shown in Figure 17.1. The GripTight mount literally grips your smartphone around the edges, and a special head lets you pan and tilt your phone while recording. In addition, the Gorillapad's legs are nice and flexible, not only for standing upright but also for wrapping around any nearby items for added stability.

FIGURE 17.1   Keep your camera steady with the GripTight Gorillapod Video tripod. (Photo courtesy Joby.)

Other popular smartphone tripods and mounts include the following:

- ▶ Breffo Spiderpodium (www.breffo.com)

- ▶ Gary Fong Flip-Cage (www.garyfongestore.com)

- ▶ iStabilizer Flex (www.istabilizer.com)

- ▶ Slingshot Universal Phone Holder and Instant Tripod (www.woxom.com)

If you have a tablet, consider the Tabflex from iStabilizer (www.istabilizer.com). Or, if you want to mount your tablet to a traditional tripod, try iStabilizer's Tabmount instead.

TIP: **Tripod Adapter**

If you already own a tripod for your digital camera, consider the SnapMount SM2 Tripod Mount (www.snapmount.com). This inexpensive adapter fastens to your smartphone and includes a standard screw mount that then attaches to your tripod.

Shooting a Better Picture with External Lighting

If your vines look dark, blurry, or pixelated, or if the color is way out of whack, then chances are you're not shooting with enough light. The lenses in most smartphones and tablets simply aren't as good as the lens in a dedicated digital camera (nor is the image sensor inside the phone or tablet), which means that your camera likely doesn't handle low-light situations very well. The result is a substandard picture, unless you're shooting in sunlight or a pretty bright room.

The solution to this problem is simple—more light! One way to do this is to move your shooting outdoors (during the daytime, anyway). You can also shine more light on your vine by turning on more room lights, or by properly aiming a nearby desk lap at the subject you're shooting.

The ultimate solution, however, is to utilize some form of professional external lighting. You have lots of choices.

For starters, consider The Kick (www.riftlabs.com/kick-overview-better-pics/), shown in Figure 17.2, an external LED light that mounts on the back of your iPhone and provides up to a thousand different lighting variations. Just dial in the type and color of light you want and the five rows of LEDs light up to deliver room-filling brightness. It's a bit pricey ($179) but an innovative approach to camera phone lighting.

FIGURE 17.2   Light better vines with The Kick, an iPhone-mounted LED light. (Photo courtesy Rift Labs.)

Also worth considering is the Pocket Spotlight (www.photojojo.com/store/awesomeness/pocket-spotlight/), shown in Figure 17.3. This battery-powered LED light attaches to the headphone jack of your smartphone or tablet and delivers up to an hour of continuous lighting. (It's also a lot less expensive than The Kick, at just $30.)

If you want even better lighting—and more control over it—utilize stand-mounted floodlights (photofloods), like those shown in Figure 17.4. Position two of these external lights in front of and to the sides of your subject, in a V configuration, and you'll achieve pro-quality lighting results. You can find a variety of photoflood kits at your local camera store, from manufacturers such as Alzo Digital (www.alzodigital.com), Bescor (www.bescor.com), Interfit (www.interfitphotographic.com), and Smith-Victor (www.smithvictor.com).

FIGURE 17.3   The Pocket Spotlight mounts to any smartphone's headphone jack. (Photo courtesy Photojojo.)

FIGURE 17.4   Use two freestanding photofloods for professional-level lighting. (Photo courtesy Alzo Digital.)

Getting a Different View with Add-On Lenses

Throughout this book we've noted the limitation of the lens built into most smartphone and tablet cameras. Fortunately, you can supplement your device's built-in lens with a variety of add-on lenses. These lenses typically fit over your device's built-in lens.

To shoot faraway subjects, use a telephoto lens. This type of lens, such as the iPhone Telephoto Lens (www.photojojo.com/store/awesomeness/iphone-telephoto-lens/) in Figure 17.5, lets you zoom in 8 to 12 times greater than normal. That brings you very close to distant action.

FIGURE 17.5   The iPhone Telephoto Lens lets you zoom into faraway scenes. (Photo courtesy Photojojo.)

To shoot small subjects up close, use a macro lens. This type of lens provides amazing close-up detail when you're shooting something tiny, like an insect. For example, the Easy Macro Cell Lens Band (www.photojojo.com/store/awesomeness/macro-lens-band/), shown in

Figure 17.6, wraps around your smartphone to provide macro shooting capability. (It only costs $15, too.)

FIGURE 17.6 The Easy Macro Cell Lens Band lets you shoot tiny objects in high detail. (Photo courtesy Photojojo.)

To shoot landscapes, use a wide angle lens. This type of lens lets you fit more of the scene into the frame, which is useful with both interior and exterior shots. (Figure 17.7 shows the dual Magnetic Mount Wide/Macro lens attached to an iPhone; learn more at www.photojojo.com/store/awesomeness/cell-phone-lenses/.)

TIP: **3-in-1**

For optimum flexibility, consider the Olloclip 3-in-1 Lens Kit (www.olloclip.com). This useful accessory includes three different lenses (wide angle, macro, and fisheye) in a single unit that snaps over your iPhone's normal lens.

If you want the best possible picture, use lenses designed for high-end digital single lens reflex (D-SLR) cameras. The iPhone SLR Mount (www.photojojo.com/store/awesomeness/iphone-slr-mount/) lets you turn your iPhone into a D-SLR camera by attaching your favorite telephoto, wide angle, or other camera lens. At $249, the SLR Mount isn't cheap, but then you can attach any Canon or Nikon D-SLR lens you might possess.

FIGURE 17.7   The Magnetic Mount Wide/Macro lens combines wide angle and macro lenses in a single unit. (Photo courtesy Photojojo.)

Creating Special Effects

Then there are various special effect lenses. For example, a fisheye lens is an ultra-wide angle lens that produces a strong visual distortion around the center of the frame. Color lenses let you emphasize different colors in a shot. Multi-image lenses produce multiple images within the frame, like looking through a multi-faceted jewel.

TIP: **9-in-1**

The Holga iPhone Lens (www.holgadirect.com) is a rotating disc that attaches over your phone's built-in lens. It provides nine different lens effects—Dual Image, Triple Image, Quadruple Image, Macro, Red Filter, Green Filter, Yellow Filter, Red Filter with Clear Center, Yellow Filter with Clear Center, Blue Filter with Clear Center, and an open hole for photos with no effect. It sells for $30.

But you don't need an expensive add-on lens to create nifty special effects. Instead, you can use common household objects in creative ways.

For example, to give a soft-focus effect, put a layer of gauzy material, such as pantyhose, over your camera's lens. Or, for a more out-of-focus effect, shoot through a bottle or piece of plastic.

Enhancing the Sound with an External Microphone

Most serious Vinesters rightly focus on improving the picture of their videos as much as possible. But with many types of vines (stop motion being a notable exception) the sound is also important—and you have to rely on your smartphone or tablet's built-in microphone to do the job. Often, that's not good enough.

The solution to crummy Vine soundtracks is to use an external microphone. Most of these mics attach via your device's 1/8-inch audio connector and provide much, much better fidelity than what you get otherwise.

If you're recording your own voice while you're shooting something else, consider using a headset with a built-in microphone. For example, Plantronics' M210c headset (www.plantronics.com), shown in Figure 17.8, puts a mini-boom noise-cancelling mic up close to your mouth for studio-like results.

When you're recording someone who's in the shot, there are even more options. The MicW iShotgun (www.mic-w.com), shown in Figure 17.9, is an an external shotgun mic that lets you zero in on the sounds you need to capture. It's perfect when you want to record someone talking in a noisy room; the shotgun mic does a great job rejecting off-axis noise. Just point and shoot, pretty much.

FIGURE 17.8 Record better-sounding narration with the Plantronics M210c headset. (Photo courtesy Plantronics.)

FIGURE 17.9 Point the MicW iShotgun at whomever is speaking to capture better audio. (Photo courtesy MicW.)

Then there's The iRig Mic (www.ikmultimedia.com/products/irigmic/), shown in Figure 17.10, which is a handheld microphone that connects to any Apple or Android device. This one is a good deal if the subject of your video is used to talking into this type of mic.

FIGURE 17.10   Put the iRig Mic in the hands of whomever's talking. (Photo courtesy IK Multimedia.)

Other Cool Accessories

There are many other useful accessories you can add to your iPhone or Android phone to enhance the quality of your Vine videos. Let's look at a few.

Adding Remote Recording

One of the challenges in shooting a Vine video, especially stop motion videos, is keeping the picture from shaking when you tap the phone's screen to record. The solution to this dilemma is to use some sort of remote trigger device, such as Belkin's LiveAction Camera Grip (www.belkin.com). This nifty little gadget, shown in Figure 17.11, functions as both an ergonomic grip for your phone and a remote shutter button. Press the black video record button to start recording, and release the button to stop. Your phone stays steady throughout.

FIGURE 17.11   Keep the camera steady when you start and stop recording with the LiveAction Camera Grip. (Photo courtesy Belkin.)

Even better, do all your starting and stopping remotely with Belkin's LiveAction Camera Remote (www.belkin.com). As you can see in Figure 17.12, this nifty little gizmo is a wireless shutter button for your phone; it works up to 30 feet away, so you never have to touch your phone to record. It's perfect for rock-steady stop motion recording. You can even use it to record yourself using your phone's rear-facing camera, by tapping the remote in your hand.

FIGURE 17.12   Start and stop recording from up to 30 feet away, with the wireless LiveAction Camera Remote. (Photo courtesy Belkin.)

Shooting Action

Want to shoot an exciting on-the-go video for Vine? Then check out the Bikepod (www.photojojo.com/store/awesomeness/bikepod/), which mounts your smartphone to the handlebars of your bicycle, as shown in Figure 17.13. You still have to tap the screen to record, but at least you don't have to hold your phone, too.

And if you're a scuba diver, you can record underwater vines. All you need is the LifeProof Case (www.lifeproof.com), which keeps your iPhone or iPad dry and is submersible up to six feet. It features a touch sensitive screen so you can tap away while recording underwater.

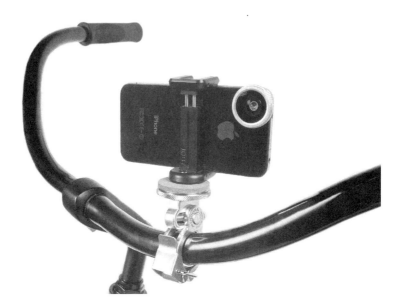

FIGURE 17.13   Shoot a vine while riding your bike with the Bikepod.
(Photo courtesy Photojojo.)

Summary

In this lesson, you learned about various accessories you can add to your
smartphone and tablet to enhance your Vine recordings.

LESSON 18

Embedding a Vine on a Web Page or Blog

In this lesson, you learn how to embed Vine videos on a web page or in a blog post.

Generating the Embed Code

Vine videos aren't just for mobile viewing. Vine lets you embed vines on any web page or in any blog post. This way, your friends who aren't yet using the Vine app can still watch the cool Vine videos you shoot.

Vine generates special HTML code for embedding any vine posted by its members. This code is emailed to you, upon request; you can then embed the code in your own web page.

> NOTE: **Any Vine**
> You can embed not just your own vines but any video posted to Vine. This lets you share videos from other Vinesters you follow.

To generate the embed code for a vine, follow these steps:

1. Navigate to the vine you want to embed.

2. Tap the More (three dots) button, shown in Figure 18.1, to display the More panel.

FIGURE 18.1   Tap the More button to begin.

3. Tap the Share This Post button to display the Share panel.

4. Tap the Embed button, shown in Figure 18.2, to display the New Message screen.

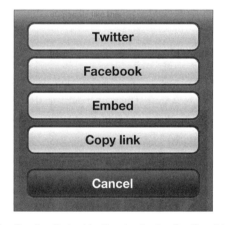

FIGURE 18.2   Tap the Embed button to display the New Message screen.

5. Enter your email address into the To: field, as shown in Figure 18.3.

6. Tap Send to send the email to yourself.

FIGURE 18.3 Enter your email address for Vine to send you a message with the embed code.

Copying the Code

The email message that Vine sends you contains the HTML code you need to embed the selected video in any web page. The email contains instructions for you to follow. In general, follow these steps:

1. Open the email message sent to you from Vine.

2. Click the link in the email message.

3. This launches your web browser and displays an Embed Post page for this video, like the one shown in Figure 18.4. You can play the video from this web page, or follow the instructions to embed it in another web page.

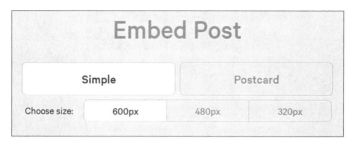

FIGURE 18.4   The Embed Post page for a Vine video.

4. To display the video with no surrounding frame, click Simple.

5. To display the video with a surrounding frame, as shown in Figure 18.5, click Postcard.

FIGURE 18.5   A vine displayed with surrounding frame (Postcard view).

6. Click the button for the size at which you want to display the video—600 px (largest), 480 px, or 320 px (smallest).

7. Scroll down and highlight the code in the text box beneath the video, as shown in Figure 18.6.

```
<iframe class="vine-embed"
src="https://vine.co/v/bLvmMUmwi2L/embed/simple" width="600"
height="600" frameborder="0"></iframe><script async
src="//platform.vine.co/static/scripts/embed.js" charset="utf-8">
</script>
```

FIGURE 18.6   Copy the embed code from the Embed Post page.

8. Right-click the selected code and select Copy from the pop-up menu.

Embedding a Vine in a Web Page

After you've copied the custom embed code, you have to paste the code in your web page's underlying HTML. To do this, you need to open the web page in your HTML editing program of choice. You can then follow these steps:

1. Position the cursor where on the web page you want the video to appear.

2. Right-click your mouse and select Paste from the pop-up menu.

3. The Vine embed code is now pasted into your web page's underlying HTML. Save the web page to display the video on your website.

Embedding a Vine in a Blog Post

Embedding the Vine code in a blog post is similar to pasting it into a web page. Follow these steps:

1. After copying the embed code as described previously, open a new blog post.

2. Click the HTML button (Blogger) or HTML tab (Wordpress) to display the underlying HTML code.

3. Position the cursor where you want the video to appear.

4. Right-click and select Paste from the pop-up menu.

5. Finish posting your blog post as normal.

The new blog post now includes the selected Vine video. Readers of your blog can click the video to begin playback.

Summary

In this lesson, you learned how to embed a Vine video on your web page or blog post.

LESSON 19

Viewing Vines on Other Sites

In this lesson, you learn how to find and view Vine videos on third-party websites.

Why Vine Isn't on the Web

Surprisingly, Vine doesn't let you view its videos on the Web. Vine's identity is as a mobile service, so that's how it intends its videos to be viewed—via the Vine mobile apps for iOS and Android.

Oh, Vine does have a website. (It's here: www.vine.co—*not* www.vine.com.) But, as you can see in Figure 19.1, it's primarily a gateway for downloading the Vine app, accessing Vine's help system, and reading about new events in the Vine blog. There is no way to find or view videos from the Vine website.

So if you want to view vines, you have to pull out your mobile device, launch the Vine mobile app, and view them that way. Shot on mobile devices, viewed on mobile devices—that's how Vine views the world.

So what do you do if you don't have your mobile device handy, or would rather watch your favorite Vine videos on your computer screen? Fortunately, where there's a will, there's a way.

FIGURE 19.1   Vine's official website—no vines for viewing here.

Finding Vines on the Web

When it comes to watching Vines on your desktop or notebook PC, there are several third-party (that is, not run by Vine) websites that aggregate Vine videos for computer users. These sites can be accessed via any web browser, on either Windows or Mac computers, and even using the web browser on your mobile device. They let you browse or search the entire database of Vine videos, then let you watch the ones you like.

Seenive

Seenive (www.seenive.com) happens to be this author's favorite Vine viewing site. That's because you're not just subjected to the latest uploads, but have the capability to both browse and search by person or hashtag.

NOTE: **Anagram**
Seenive is an anagram of "see vine."

The Seenive home page features today's best vines at the top, and beneath that is a three-column affair. As you can see in Figure 19.2, the first column displays Hot Viners, the middle one Popular Vines, and the last one Trending Hashtags. Click any person's name to view their vines; click any vine thumbnail to view that video on its own web page.

FIGURE 19.2   Viewing vines, "Viners," and hashtags on Seenive.

The Seenive site offers several different sections, accessible from buttons along the top navigation bar. Here's what you get:

- ▶ **Explore.** This page lets you browse popular people, tags, and products. It also offers a search box for finding specific people or vines.

- ▶ **Popular.** This page displays the Best of Vine—the most popular vines of the moment.

- ▶ **Editor's Picks.** This page displays Vine's Editor's Picks— literally, those vines handpicked by Vine's editors.

- ▶ **More.** Click this option to learn more about Seenive.

Click the Seenive logo to return to the home page.

Even better, you can search Seenive for specific vines and Vinesters. Enter a name or tag into the Search People box and you see the Explore page for that query, as shown in Figure 19.3. From there you can filter the results to display matching People, Tags, and Products.

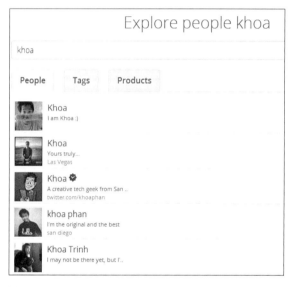

FIGURE 19.3   Searching for people, tags, and products with Seenive.

Vinebox

Vinebox (www.vinebox.co) displays a grid of Vine's most recent videos on its home page, as shown in Figure 19.4. Click any vine to view it in a larger panel superimposed on the home screen.

You can also search Vinebox for people or tags. Just enter a name or tag into the Search box, press Enter, and then browse through the search results.

FIGURE 19.4   Viewing a collage of vines on Vinebox.

Vines Map

Vines Map (www.vinesmap.com) is an unusual vine viewer in that it literally puts vines on the map. This site uses OpenStreetMap data to display geotagged vines on a world map, as shown in Figure 19.5, based on where they were shot. Zoom in and then click anywhere on the map to view vines from that specific location—or wait for Vines Map to show you another video somewhere else around the world.

VineRoulette

The home page of VineRoulette (www.vineroulette.com) lets you browse the most popular Vine hashtags or search for specific tags or people. When you click a tag or perform a search, you're presented with a real time collage of matching vines, like the one shown in Figure 19.6. Mouse over a vine to view it (the thumbnail image enlarges slightly) and read its text description.

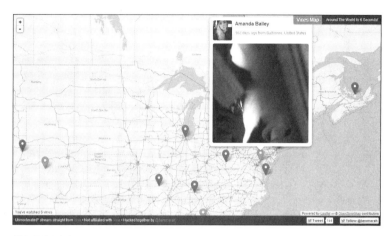

FIGURE 19.5   Viewing vines by location with Vines Map.

FIGURE 19.6   Viewing VineRoulette's collage of vines.

VinesZap

VinesZap (www.vineszap.com) displays the latest posts on Vine. By default, videos appear four to a page, as shown in Figure 19.7, with all four playing simultaneously. You can change the layout to display just a single video or a nine-video grid.

FIGURE 19.7   Viewing a grid of recent vines on VinesZap.

The videos displayed on VinesZap are continuously changing. Watch for a minute or two and you see new videos appear where old ones once were. So you see a continuously changing grid of videos, keeping you up to date with the most recent posts. Click a video to view it on its own screen.

Vpeeker

Vpeeker (www.vpeeker.com), formerly known as Vinepeek, was one of the first third-party sites available for viewing Vine videos. As you can see in Figure 19.8, the Vpeeker home page shows a single vine, although the vine displays is continuously changing. Over the course of a minute you'll see a handful of different videos; if you don't like what you see, wait a bit and it will change. It's totally random.

One of the unique things about Vpeeker is that it lets you "save" your favorite vines for later viewing, and for sharing via Facebook. To start saving vines, click the camera button; the vines you save are displayed in the top-right corner of the screen. To view a saved vine, just click its title. To share it, click the Facebook icon.

FIGURE 19.8   Viewing a feed of the most recent vines on Vpeeker.

CAUTION: **Single Session**

Vpeeker's saved vines are saved only for your current viewing session. Your "saved" list will clear when you leave the Vpeeker site for another web page.

Summary

In this lesson, you learned about several third-party sites that let you view vines on your personal computer.

LESSON 20

Downloading Vines

In this lesson, you learn how to download and save Vine videos to your computer—as well as convert them to animated GIF files.

Saving a Vine to Your Computer

What do you do when you see a vine that you'd like to watch again—preferably on your home computer? The solution is to download that video and then watch it using your computer's media player software.

Downloading a vine is a somewhat convoluted practice, if only because Vine doesn't make it easy to display its videos on your computer screen. (Vine is primarily a mobile app and service, remember.) There is a way to do it, but you have to carefully adhere to the following steps:

1. From the Vine app on your mobile device, navigate to the vine you'd like to save.

2. Tap the More (three dots) button, shown in Figure 20.1, to display the More pane.

3. Tap the Share This Post button to display the Share pane.

4. Tap the Embed button to display the New Message screen.

5. Enter your email address into the To: field.

6. Tap Send to send the email message.

7. On your computer, go to your email inbox and open the new email message.

8. Click the link in the message to display the video's Embed Post page in your web browser.

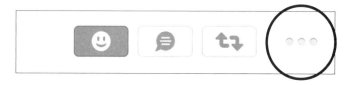

FIGURE 20.1 Tap the More button to access sharing options.

9. Go to your browser's address box and delete the **/embed** from the end of the URL, then press Enter. For example, if the Embed Post page's URL was **www.vine.co/v/bYQhLL0ijYt/embed**, change it to **www.vine.co/v/bYQhLL0ijYt**.

10. This displays the viewing page for that vine, as shown in Figure 20.2. Right-click the video and select Save Video As from the pop-up menu.

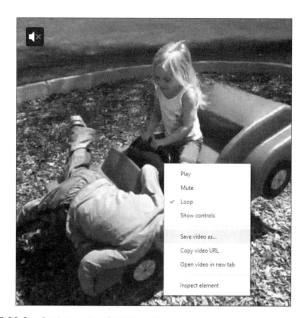

FIGURE 20.2 Saving a vine from its viewing page.

11. When the Save As dialog box appears, as shown in Figure 20.3, select a location for the video.

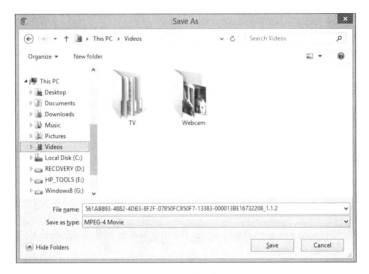

FIGURE 20.3   Saving a vine as an MPEG-4 file.

12. If you want to give the video a more descriptive name (as opposed to the numeric gobbledy gook supplied by Vine), enter that name into the File Name box.

13. Click the Save button.

The video is saved as an MPEG-4 (.MP4) file on your computer's hard drive. You can now open the video with your media player program of choice. (If you're running Windows, for example, use Windows Media Player to play the newly saved vine.)

Converting a Vine to an Animated GIF

When you use the preceding procedure to save a Vine video as an MPEG-4 file, that video runs its six-second maximum when you press the

Play button and then it stops. You can, however, convert any Vine video you've downloaded into a self-running, continuous-loop GIF animation. The GIF file can then be embedded on a web page or blog post, or even linked to from a tweet or Facebook update.

To convert a vine to a GIF file, follow these steps:

1. From the Vine app on your mobile device, navigate to the vine you'd like to save.

2. Tap the More button to display the More pane.

3. Tap the Share This Post button to display the Share pane.

4. Tap the Embed button to display the New Message screen.

5. Enter your email address into the To: field.

6. Tap Send to send the email message.

7. On your computer, go to your email inbox and open the new email message.

8. Click the link in the message to display the video's Embed Post page in your web browser.

9. Go to your browser's address box and delete the **/embed** from the end of the URL, then press Enter.

10. Select and right-click the new URL and select Copy from the pop-up menu. Make sure you've selected the entire URL, including the **http://** at the beginning.

11. From your web browser, go to the GIF Vine website (www.gifvine.co), shown in Figure 20.4.

12. Right-click in the Gimme a Vine URL box and select Paste from the pop-up menu.

13. Click the Make This Vine a Gif! button.

FIGURE 20.4   Converting a Vine video into an animated GIF with GIF Vine.

14. GIF Vine now displays your vine as an animated GIF. To download the GIF file, right-click the image and select Save Picture As or Save Image As.

15. When the Save As dialog box appears, select a location for the file and click Save.

The vine is saved as an GIF file on your computer's hard drive. You can now view that file with any photo viewer or editor program, and use the file as you deem fit.

Summary

In this lesson, you learned how to save Vine videos to your computer and how to convert them to animated GIF files.

Uploading Videos Not Shot with the Vine App

In this lesson, you learn how to hack your smartphone to upload existing videos to Vine.

Is the Vine App the Only Way to Upload Videos to Vine?

As you've learned throughout this book, you upload videos to Vine using the Vine mobile app. You shoot the video using the app on your mobile phone or tablet, and then upload the video directly from the app to the Vine service.

What about videos you've shot otherwise? Say you have a short video you shot with your iPhone's built-in video camera, and have stored in your phone's library. Is there any way to upload that existing video to Vine?

By default, the answer is no. Vine is designed to use videos shot exclusively with the Vine mobile app.

However, there is a way to "hack" the Vine app to enable it to upload videos you've already shot and stored on your mobile device. You can only do this with videos that are six seconds or less in length, of course. And it requires a bit of work and the use of two third-party utilities to trick Vine into accepting a non-Vine video.

All that said, this hack enables you to upload even more creative videos to your Vine account. Because you can upload any six-second video using this method, you can employ all manner of post-production editing and special effects, which are not possible with the standard Vine app. It gives you even more creative control over the videos you share via Vine.

> NOTE: **Custom Vines for Business**
>
> If you're using Vine to market your brand or product, the ability to retain more creative control is appealing. For this reason, many companies are using this approach to produce more professional-looking videos outside the Vine app and then upload them to their Vine accounts.

Uploading an Existing Video to Vine

To upload your own custom video to Vine, you need a video that conforms to specific Vine technical standards and a handful of third-party utilities. You also need to be technically comfortable with "hacking" into and editing the files stored on your mobile device.

What You Need

Before you get started, assemble the following tools:

- ▶ A six-second (max) video in the correct video format (see the following section)

- ▶ A video editing program, such as Adobe Photoshop Elements, to edit your video (optional)

- ▶ A video encoding program, such as HandBrake

- ▶ A file management program for your computer and mobile device, such as iExplorer

- ▶ The vine mobile app

Creating and Editing the Video

You can shoot your video using any video camera, not just the one built into your smartphone or tablet. You can shoot multiple short videos, if you like, with the goal of editing them together into a single master video.

When you're done shooting, transfer the video file(s) from your mobile device to your personal computer. You can then edit the video in any video editing program, such as Adobe Photoshop Elements or iMovie. Use the video editing program to edit together multiple shots, apply transitions (such as fades and wipes) between shots, add onscreen text and graphics, and apply a variety of special effects.

When you're done editing, be sure to save the video as an MP4 file. Also, make sure the video is no more than six seconds long, and has a square aspect ratio of 480 pixels x 480 pixels. (This might require some cropping of the video in the editing app, as most videos are shot in a wider aspect ratio.)

TIP: **Aspect Ratio**

Because most video cameras record in a wider screen format than the square format preferred by Vine, you might need to either crop your original video or letterbox it (shrink it so that black bars appear on the top and bottom of the video).

Encoding the Video

After you've used a video editing program to edit and save the video, you now have to properly encode it for Vine. All videos uploaded to Vine have to match the following technical specifications:

- ▶ Length: 6 seconds or less
- ▶ Picture size: 480 x 480 pixels
- ▶ File format: MP4
- ▶ Video codec: H.264

▶ Frame rate: 30 fps (frames per second), constant frame rate

▶ Average bit rate: 500 bps (bits per second)

▶ Audio format: AAC mono

▶ Audio bit rate: 128 bps

▶ Audio sample rate: 44.1 kHz (kilohertz)

NOTE: **Match the Specs**

Your video has to match these specifications because Vine is designed to work with videos that are all identical, from a technical perspective. If your video does not match any of these specs, Vine won't recognize it and it will be rejected.

You typically encode the video using an encoding/transcoding software program, such as HandBrake. Follow these steps:

NOTE: **HandBrake**

HandBrake is a free, open source program that can convert videos from practically any format to any other format. Learn more about and download HandBrake at www.handbrake.fr.

---

1. From within HandBrake, click Source and then select Open File to select the video file to encode.

2. Go to the Destination section, shown in Figure 21.1, and enter a name for the output file into the File field.

3. Go to the Output settings section, pull down the Container control, and select MP4.

4. Select the Picture tab and make sure Width is set to 480.

5. Select the Video tab, as shown in Figure 21.2, and set Video Codec to H.264.

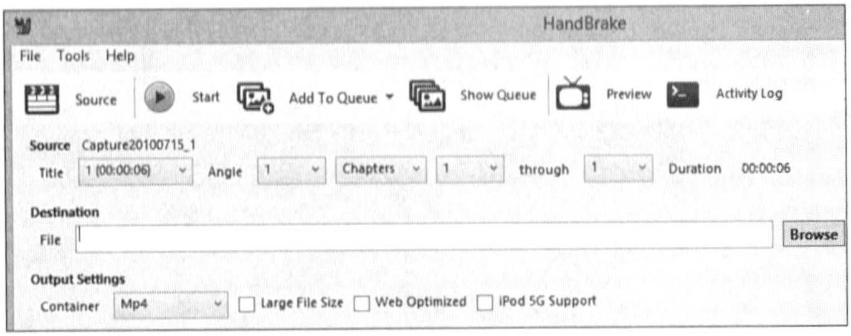

FIGURE 21.1   Configuring output settings in HandBrake.

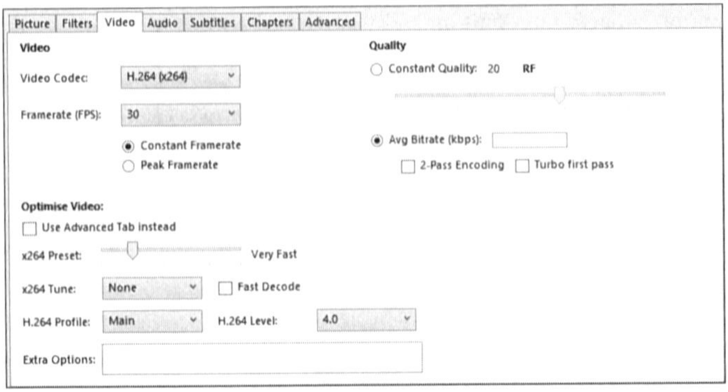

FIGURE 21.2   Configuring video settings in HandBrake.

6. Set Framerate to 30, and select Constant Framerate.

7. Select Avg Bitrate and enter **500** as the value.

8. Select the Audio tab, shown in Figure 21.3, pull down the Codec control, and select AAC (faac).

9. Pull down the Bitrate control and select 128.

10. Pull down the Samplerate control and select 44.1.

11. Pull down the Mixdown control and select Mono.

12. Click the green Start button to encode the file.

FIGURE 21.3   Configuring audio settings in HandBrake.

Recording a Dummy Vine

For this hack to work, you have to replace a regular Vine video with the custom video you've just encoded. The way to do this is to shoot a "dummy" video—but don't upload it just yet. Follow these steps:

1. On your mobile device, open the Vine app and record about five seconds of video. Do *not* press the right arrow to finalize the vine.

2. Exit the Vine app without completing the video.

This stores a copy of your in-process vine in your device's photo/video library.

Replacing the Dummy Vine

The key to uploading your custom video is to replace the in-progess vine with your own video file. Vine will think that your file is the standard vine you started to record and upload it. Your custom video will then appear alongside all the videos on the Vine service.

> NOTE: **iExplorer**
>
> iExplorer is a software program you use to manage the files on your iPhone or iPad from your personal computer. The full version runs $35, but the free trial version works just fine for this file replacement process. Learn more and download iExplorer from www.macroplant.com/iexplorer/.

To transfer your custom vine to your mobile device, you use a file management program such as iExplorer. Follow these steps:

1. Connect your mobile device to your computer.

2. Open iExplorer or another file management program of choice.

3. Copy your custom video into the TMP folder on your mobile device.

4. Look for the file that starts **temp_record_*12345***, which is the in-progress Vine video you started recording. (In this instance, *12345* will be replaced by a different number, assigned specifically to this video.) Rename this file **x_temp_record_*12345***.

5. Rename your custom video to the original vine's file name: **temp_record_*12345*** (without the **x_** in front of it).

You have now replaced the original temporary video file with your custom video file. (The original temporary video is also saved, in case you want to access it again.)

Uploading Your Custom Video

With your custom video file in place, it's time to complete the recording process and upload that video to Vine. Follow these steps:

1. Launch the Vine app on your mobile device. It should start up with your in-progress video ready to be finalized.

2. Press the right arrow to finalize the vine.

3. Follow the normal steps to describe and upload the vine.

Your custom video should now be uploaded to your Vine feed and shared with all your followers.

NOTE: **No Guarantees**

Because uploading existing videos in this fashion goes against how Vine works and supersedes Vine's standard processes, there is no guarantee that the custom videos you upload will always work. Although many users have found success with this approach, others have found that their videos do not appear on the Vine service, or appear for a short period of time and are then taken down (presumably by Vine). In other words, your mileage may vary.

Summary

In this lesson, you learned how to "hack" Vine to upload custom videos you produce outside of the Vine app.

Vine Do's and Don'ts

In this lesson, you learn the right and wrong ways to post videos on Vine.

Do These Things

Vine doesn't have a lot of rules and regulations. There aren't even formal guidelines per se. But there are some things you should do if you want to be accepted into the Vine community, have your vines viewed by others, and gain Vine followers.

Think Visually

Vine is a visual medium; it's all about videos, after all. So when it comes to determining what kinds of things to post, you have to think visually. That is, your vines need to reflect content that can be expressed visually. Or, put in the reverse, you should avoid creating vines that address content that does not have a visual component.

What is visual content? Anything you can show. In contrast, non-visual content is something you have to tell people about. If you have to describe it with words (either written or verbal), it isn't suited to Vine.

Comparing different types of leaves is something best done visually, ideally suited to the Vine environment. Comparing the writing styles of Hemingway and Steinbeck, on the other hand, isn't visual at all and probably not a good subject for a Vine video. Choose your subjects based on how visual they are.

Post What's Interesting to You— and To Others

Vine is all about expressing yourself in six seconds or less. You don't want to waste those precious seconds on something that isn't that terribly interesting.

What makes a video interesting? Start with what interests you. If you find something compelling or appealing, chances are others will, too. If it makes you laugh, it'll probably make your friends laugh, as well. Use your own interests to determine what types of vines to create.

Even better, make sure your vines appeal to the people you want to follow you. If your followers tend to like cute cat videos, then give them cute cat videos. If your friends like stop motion construction paper videos, go the stop motion construction paper route. But don't serve up stop motion construction paper videos to your cute cat-loving friends—unless you can make cute cats out of construction paper, that is.

Describe Your Vine

Vines are visual, but they don't stand on their own. You need to describe your vines so that people will know what they're about to watch. A vine's description is also how it gets found when people are searching for videos to watch. Every vine you upload needs a concise, accurate description.

It doesn't hurt if your descriptions are also fun to read. Just because a description is concise doesn't mean that it has to be dry. You'll attract more viewers if you use a little humor to describe your vines.

For that matter, use the description to set up the vine. Given Vine's six-second limitation, you might want to get things started with a one- or two-sentence setup. For example, if your vine shows how to boil an egg, set things up with a description that starts with "How to boil an egg." That way you don't have to waste precious seconds within the vine saying "This is how you boil an egg." Make your description work with your video to create a complete package.

Use Popular Hashtags

When it comes to getting your videos found in Vine's search results, hashtags matter. Pop in a few hashtags throughout your description that link to topics people are likely to be searching for. You'll get more viewers if your vines are tied into popular hashtags.

You can include hashtags within the body of your description (such as **How to boil an #egg**), or at the end of your description (**How to boil an egg. #eggboil**). Either approach is valid.

> NOTE: **Trending Hashtags**
> Stay on top of what's popular by going to the Explore screen in the Vine app. Scroll to the bottom of the screen to see Trending Tags—the hottest hashtags on Vine at this moment.

Be Social—Like, Follow, and Comment

Vine is a social network. To get the most out of Vine, you need to be social. That means becoming a willing and active participant in Vine's social functions.

In practice, that means getting out there and watching lots of vines from other Vinesters. When you find a vine you like, like it. When you find a vine that's particularly interesting, comment on it or revine it. When you find a Vinester who's posted a lot of videos you like, follow him.

The more you participate, the more likely it will be that others will take a chance and watch your Vine videos. Participation enhances viewership. After all, you can't expect people to follow you if you don't follow them, too.

Don't Do These Things

Like I said, there aren't a lot of hard and fast rules for Vining. Still, there are some activities you probably should avoid.

Don't Try to Fit Too Much Into Six Seconds

There's only such much stuff you can cram into a six-second video. Some things just don't lend themselves to that time limitation.

For example, you probably can't explain how to learn to fly an airplane in six seconds, so you shouldn't do it. Likewise, summarizing Proust or detailing the history of Islam are things that will probably take longer than six seconds. They're not ideal Vine topics.

Pick topics that you can easily fit into Vine's six-second timeframe. Avoid those that six seconds won't let you do justice to. It's that simple.

Don't Over Post

How often should you post to Vine? Vine isn't like Twitter or Facebook, both of which demand multiple posts per day. Trust me, if you try to post a dozen Vines in a single afternoon, not only will you find that physically and mentally challenging, you'll also wear out your followers. Even if you produce really interesting and creative videos, if you post too many of them, people will get tired of you.

What's the right posting frequency? Again, there are no set rules, but if you post once a week or so, you're doing good. Post more frequently only when you have something interesting to post. Don't post if you don't have anything of interest to your followers.

Don't Post Objectionable Content

When it comes to deciding what to post, avoid content that could be offensive to others. Admittedly, Vine had initial appeal to young people posting selfies of their genitals (it's an Instagram that moves!), but Vine quickly banned hashtags and searches for the most obvious pornographic terms. So while there are still nasty vines out there, they're very difficult to find.

Vine's terms of service quite obviously ban certain types of content. Here's what the TOS says:

> We reserve the right at all times (but will not have an obligation) to remove or refuse to distribute any Content on the Services and to suspend or terminate users or reclaim usernames without liability to you. You may not post Content that:
>
> ► Impersonates another person or entity in a manner that does or is intended to mislead, confuse, or deceive others;
>
> ► Violates the rights of a third party, including copyright, trademark, privacy, and publicity rights;
>
> ► Is a direct and specific threat of violence to others;
>
> ► Is furtherance of illegal activities; or
>
> ► Is harassing, abusive, or constitutes spam.

Although Vine doesn't specifically ban adult or violent content, you won't necessarily get a lot of followers for those kinds of videos. Stick to topics that don't offend and you'll reach a wider audience.

Don't Steal

Note the second bullet in the terms of service just referenced: Vine says you can't post content that violates "copyright, trademark, privacy, and publicity rights." In effect, this says that you can't include someone else's content in your Vine videos.

So you can't take a video you found elsewhere and upload it to Vine as your own. You also can't appropriate music or video content from other sources within your videos. So having a Jay-Z track play in the background of your video is actually copyright infringement and not allowed. For that matter, shooting a video of your TV playing the latest episode of *Breaking Bad* is also out of bounds.

Bottom line, if you didn't make it yourself, don't upload it. It's not yours to do so.

Summary

In this lesson, you learned the do's and don'ts of Vine etiquette.

Index

X–Y–Z

W

SamsTeachYourself

from Sams Publishing

Sams Teach Yourself in 10 Minutes offers straightforward, practical answers for fast results.

These small books of 250 pages or less offer tips that point out shortcuts and solutions, cautions that help you avoid common pitfalls, and notes that explain additional concepts and provide additional information. By working through the 10-minute lessons, you learn everything you need to know quickly and easily!

When you only have time for the answers, Sams Teach Yourself books are your best solution.

Visit **informit.com/samsteachyourself** for a complete listing of the products available.

Sams Publishing is a Pearson brand and part of the family of bestselling technology publishers.

 THE TRUSTED TECHNOLOGY LEARNING SOURCE

 PEARSON

 Addison-Wesley   Cisco Press   EXAM/CRAM   IBM Press.   QUE   PRENTICE HALL   SAMS   Safari

SAMS

REGISTER

THIS PRODUCT

informit.com/register

Register the Addison-Wesley, Exam Cram, Prentice Hall, Que, and Sams products you own to unlock great benefits.

To begin the registration process, simply go to **informit.com/register** to sign in or create an account. You will then be prompted to enter the 10- or 13-digit ISBN that appears on the back cover of your product.

Registering your products can unlock the following benefits:

- Access to supplemental content, including bonus chapters, source code, or project files.
- A coupon to be used on your next purchase.

Registration benefits vary by product. Benefits will be listed on your Account page under Registered Products.

About InformIT — THE TRUSTED TECHNOLOGY LEARNING SOURCE

INFORMIT IS HOME TO THE LEADING TECHNOLOGY PUBLISHING IMPRINTS Addison-Wesley Professional, Cisco Press, Exam Cram, IBM Press, Prentice Hall Professional, Que, and Sams. Here you will gain access to quality and trusted content and resources from the authors, creators, innovators, and leaders of technology. Whether you're looking for a book on a new technology, a helpful article, timely newsletters, or access to the Safari Books Online digital library, InformIT has a solution for you.

informIT.com | Addison-Wesley | Cisco Press | Exam Cram
IBM Press | Que | Prentice Hall | Sams

THE TRUSTED TECHNOLOGY LEARNING SOURCE | SAFARI BOOKS ONLINE

informIT.com

THE TRUSTED TECHNOLOGY LEARNING SOURCE

InformIT is a brand of Pearson and the online presence for the world's leading technology publishers. It's your source for reliable and qualified content and knowledge, providing access to the top brands, authors, and contributors from the tech community.

Addison-Wesley   **Cisco Press**   EXAM/**CRAM**   **IBM** Press.   QUe°   **PRENTICE HALL**   **SAMS**   Safari°

LearnIT at InformIT

Looking for a book, eBook, or training video on a new technology? Seeking timely and relevant information and tutorials? Looking for expert opinions, advice, and tips? **InformIT has the solution.**

- Learn about new releases and special promotions by subscribing to a wide variety of newsletters.
  Visit **informit.com/newsletters**.

- Access FREE podcasts from experts at **informit.com/podcasts**.

- Read the latest author articles and sample chapters at **informit.com/articles**.

- Access thousands of books and videos in the Safari Books Online digital library at **safari.informit.com**.

- Get tips from expert blogs at **informit.com/blogs**.

Visit **informit.com/learn** to discover all the ways you can access the hottest technology content.

Are You Part of the IT Crowd?

Connect with Pearson authors and editors via RSS feeds, Facebook, Twitter, YouTube, and more! Visit **informit.com/socialconnect**.

informIT.com

THE TRUSTED TECHNOLOGY LEARNING SOURCE

PEARSON

Addison-Wesley   **Cisco Press**   EXAM/**CRAM**   **IBM** Press.   QUe°   **PRENTICE HALL**   **SAMS**   Safari°

Try Safari Books Online FREE for 15 days
Get online access to Thousands of Books and Videos

Safari Books Online

FREE 15-DAY TRIAL + 15% OFF*
informit.com/safaritrial

> ## Feed your brain
> Gain unlimited access to thousands of books and videos about technology, digital media and professional development from O'Reilly Media, Addison-Wesley, Microsoft Press, Cisco Press, McGraw Hill, Wiley, WROX, Prentice Hall, Que, Sams, Apress, Adobe Press and other top publishers.

> ## See it, believe it
> Watch hundreds of expert-led instructional videos on today's hottest topics.

WAIT, THERE'S MORE!

> ## Gain a competitive edge
> Be first to learn about the newest technologies and subjects with Rough Cuts pre-published manuscripts and new technology overviews in Short Cuts.

> ## Accelerate your project
> Copy and paste code, create smart searches that let you know when new books about your favorite topics are available, and customize your library with favorites, highlights, tags, notes, mash-ups and more.

* Available to new subscribers only. Discount applies to the Safari Library and is valid for first 12 consecutive monthly billing cycles. Safari Library is not available in all countries.

Michael Miller

Sams Teach Yourself
Vine™
in **10**
Minutes

SAMS

FREE
Online Edition

Safari
Books Online

Your purchase of **Sams Teach Yourself Vine™ in 10 Minutes** includes access to a free online edition for 45 days through the **Safari Books Online** subscription service. Nearly every Sams book is available online through **Safari Books Online**, along with thousands of books and videos from publishers such as Addison-Wesley Professional, Cisco Press, Exam Cram, IBM Press, O'Reilly Media, Prentice Hall, Que, and VMware Press.

Safari Books Online is a digital library providing searchable, on-demand access to thousands of technology, digital media, and professional development books and videos from leading publishers. With one monthly or yearly subscription price, you get unlimited access to learning tools and information on topics including mobile app and software development, tips and tricks on using your favorite gadgets, networking, project management, graphic design, and much more.

Activate your FREE Online Edition at
informit.com/safarifree

STEP 1: Enter the coupon code: BRDMOGA.

STEP 2: New Safari users, complete the brief registration form.
Safari subscribers, just log in.

If you have difficulty registering on Safari or accessing the online edition,
please e-mail customer-service@safaribooksonline.com